Sarah E.V. Emery

Seven Financial Conspiracies Which Have Enslaved the

American People

Sarah E.V. Emery

Seven Financial Conspiracies Which Have Enslaved the American People

ISBN/EAN: 9783744727471

Printed in Europe, USA, Canada, Australia, Japan

Cover: Foto ©Suzi / pixelio.de

More available books at **www.hansebooks.com**

SEVEN
FINANCIAL CONSPIRACIES

WHICH HAVE

BY

MRS. SARAH E.V. EMERY.

" The great debt that capitalists will see to it is made out of the war, must be used as a measure to control the volume of money.
—*Hazzard Circular.*

IN MEMORY
OF
MY SAINTED FATHER,

WHO, FORESEEING THE RESULTS OF OUR CIVIL WAR,
AND THE CONDITIONS THAT MUST ARISE
FROM THE CORRUPT FINANCIAL SYSTEM
ADOPTED IN ITS EARLY STAGES,
GAVE WARNING TO HIS CHILDREN, ENTREATING THEM
EVER TO REMEMBER THE CAUSE OF THE OPPRESSED,
AND EVER TO CONDEMN A SYSTEM OF LEGISLATION
CALCULATED TO REDUCE THE LABORING
CLASSES TO A STATE OF ABJECT
AND HOPELESS SERVITUDE ;
IN REMEMBRANCE OF HIS PROPHETIC WORDS,
AND HIS GREAT LOVE FOR HUMANITY,
THIS LITTLE VOLUME IS SACREDLY
DEDICATED
TO THE ENSLAVED PEOPLE
OF A
DYING REPUBLIC.

Sarah Emery

SEVEN FINANCIAL CONSPIRACIES

PREFACE.

Would I add another to the multiplicity of books that is flooding the country ? Why not ? It is only a little book I offer, but it contains truths which if understood by the masses, would tend to awaken them to the dangers which threaten our free institutions. " Eternal vigilance is the price of liberty," and a people too indifferent or to self-satisfied to be mindful of their liberties are unworthy of such a boon.

Republics are lost because their guardians—the people—entrust them to scheming politicians. We did not profit by the experience of other Republics, but followed in their footsteps,—and in their downfall we see our pending doom. That such a doom may be averted, I believe to be the desire of every patriotic citizen ; and if, in the perusal of these pages, my readers are awakened to a consciousness of impending danger, I shall feel that this labor has not been in vain. A revolution is upon us. Let us see to it that it is wrought by ballots, rather than bullets.

S. E. V. E.

Preface To Two Hundred And Twentieth Thousand Edition.

Four years ago it was with many misgivings that I presented " Seven Financial Conspiracies " to the public. Would it be received with contempt or would the masses comprehend its plain though startling truths, were problems that I felt myself unable to solve. But the rapidly increasing demand for the book has been more than a satisfactory answer to my doubtful questionings. The cordial greeting which the little messenger has received from every State and Territory in the Union is indeed gratifying, for the profound interest manifested in its teachings gives assurance that the principles of justice are deeply rooted in the hearts of the American people. Scores of times have I been assured that the startling truths presented in this little book have revolutionized entire counties.

While I am gratified that such happy results have been brought about through its teachings, I take to myself but little credit for the good that has been accomplished.

This little work is but the reflection of a wonderful luminary from the pen of one of the purest philanthropists of this age—Col. B.S. Heath. For years I was a student of his inestimable book, " Labor and Finance Revolution," and sat a disciple at his feet until I became most thoroughly imbued with the spirit of his teachings.

To B.S. Heath this country owes a debt of gratitude that can never be paid until his teachings become so thoroughly incorporated into the life of every American citizen that he will know no duty higher than that of overthrowing the monopolistic powers that threaten the life of this nation.

S. E. V. E.

NOTE.—Col. Benjamin S. Heath's book, " Labor and Finance Revolution." can be obtained by sending $1.00 to his widow, Mrs. Louisa M, Heath, 1081 W. Monroe St., Chicago, Ill.

CHAPTER I.
THE CIVIL WAR PRELIMINARY TO AN INFAMOUS PLOT.

THE Earl of Chatham, England's great statesman, once said, " Show me the laws of a country and I will show you the condition of its people."

Starting upon this proposition, we are led to the conclusion that the laws of our country are not in accordance with the principles of justice and equality, for there is nothing in the condition of the masses that denotes prosperity, but rather a tendency to poverty and demoralization. No period of our history has been marked by such general dissatisfaction.

Wherever we turn is discontent ; labor idle, or at least working on short time and low pay ; mill after mill silent ; furnaces cold and unproductive ; tramps filling our highways ; the gaunt wolf of starvation staring into desolate homes, and strikes against starvation wages—those forerunners of revolution springing up on every hand. On the other side, we see granaries bursting with the abundance with which God has fattened the land, palatial mansions rising in fabulous magnificence, and mountains of wealth—the product of half-requited labor—poured into the coffers of the idle and affluent. All over the land the wail of distress comes up from poverty-stricken homes crushing out the manhood and womanhood of human kind, blighting the beauty and buoyancy of youth, and destroying the faith of mankind in an all-wise merciful father. In a land of plenty, where the willing hand of industry has created untold wealth, why should that hand be paralyzed for want of the very wealth it has created ? Why should comfortable food, clothing and homes be denied to those who have produced these things in such abundance ? Reader, these are questions that must soon be answered before the tribunal of a long-suffering but much enduring people.

In view of these facts and the responsibilities that rest upon us as American citizens, I earnestly ask that you lay aside your prejudices, and with me briefly consider a few of the circumstances that have brought about this deplorable condition. It is within the memory of many of my readers when millionaires were not indigenous to American soil. But that period has passed, and today we boast more millionaires than any other country on the globe ; tramps have increased in a geometrical ratio ; while strikes, riots and anarchists' trials constitute an exciting topic of conversation in all classes of society. There is no doubt but that the unequal distribution of the products of labor is one of the most fruitful sources of social and political disturbances.

Any rational person must admit that a nation's prosperity does not lie so much in the amount of its wealth as in a just distribution of that wealth among those who have produced it.

That nation is the most prosperous whose laborers hold warranty deeds, rather than leases of their homes, and a hundred cottage homes and gardens owned by a hundred workingmen is greater evidence of national prosperity than a million of property in the hands of a single individual. The ownership of home is the great safeguard of liberty, and it is impossible for a people long to remain free who do not own their homes. History bears us out in this statement, and we trace with minuteness the connection between land monopoly and national death. God has implanted in the human heart an unquenchable thirst for knowledge and for liberty, a knowledge of that liberty which makes men free from the bondage of their physical necessities and breaks the manacles of that slavery which through all ages, the strong have imposed upon the weaker portion of mankind.

Since the day that Esau sold his birthright for a mess of pottage, crafty men have taken advantage of the physical necessities of their less artful brothers ; since that day, too, hungry men have been selling the birthright of their liberty for a mess of pottage which barely enables them to eke out a miserable existence. From the days of Esau to the present time two classes of people have existed upon this earth, the one class who live by honest labor, the other who live off of honest labor. From earliest times the one class have lived by tilling the soil, raising flocks and herds, delving in mines, working in wood, brass and iron, or deriving their subsistance from the waters over which God had given them do minion. The other class consisted of roving bandits, who under chiefs or leaders subsisted by swooping down upon and plundering the honest toilers ; sometimes a strong band would take possession of a rich territory, subdue its people and divide the spoils between themselves ; the chief became king, the brigands nobility, and the conquered people who only the day before were happy possessors of homes, became the slaves of this robber band who ruthlessly wrenched from them their homes and the products of their toil.

Today the same two classes exist as of old, not only in Europe but in this America, which gave such glorious promise of protection to its toiling people. True, the robber chiefs of our times have not by physical force taken possession of our toilers, and the products of their labor ; they did not swoop down upon these people with bayonets and bowie knives ; they did not say to them we have conquered your country and you are our slaves ; ah, no, the terms robber and brigand are too harsh ; civilization has advanced, and these terms are obnoxious to the refined intelligence of the age. The civilized brigandage of today is ashamed of its ancestry, but its appetite for plunder is no less ravenous and daring. Modern brigandage is carried on under more euphonious titles, and new methods of robbery are employed. Instead of " robber king " and " brigand chief " we have today the money king, the coal king, the cattle king, the railroad magnate, the telegraph monopolist and the lumber baron. Instead of spoils and plunders, we have interests, dividends, revenues and rents.

The system of American government as instituted by our fathers afforded little if any opportunity for robbery and oppression. Having successfully repelled their enemies across the water their prowess was established, and the civilized world stood in awe of the young republic. Not a crowned head of Europe aspired to clip the wings of the young American eagle, and for fourscore years the proud bird soared defiantly through the American heavens, or hovered above the sacred temple of our liberties. But, alas, in an evil hour the tempter came, the guardians were betrayed, and the very sanctuary of our liberties became the charnal-house of American freedom, and the market place of American honor.

Thirty years ago the American laborer was a prospective lord. He saw within his reach a home of plenty for his family, and an old age of comfort for himself. The bright picture before him inspired industry, economy and sobriety, and the laborer was a peaceful, sober, respected citizen. The condition of the American people less than half a century ago is graphically portrayed by Chas. Dickens, who, visiting in this country in 1842, wrote from Boston to a friend in London : " There is not a man in this town nor in this State who has not a blazing fire, and meat every day for dinner, nor would a flaming sword in the air attract more attention than a beggar in the streets." But today what is the outlook for the wage-worker of this country ? He sees before him only toil, unremitting, half-requited toil ; hope dies out in his bosom, despondency takes possession of his heart ; and unless sustained by a strong faith and a giant will he breaks beneath the weight of oppression, seeks relief in a suicide's grave, or worse still attempts to drown his grief in the intoxicating cup and finally drifts into the great army of inebriates.

We are now led to the question, wherefore this amazing change in the condition of the working classes of this country ? There is a solution to this problem. As I have before stated the American system of government afforded little or no opportunity for robbery and oppression, but the vast plains and teeming valleys of this grand republic, with its innumerable sources of wealth, and millions of industrious population, was a coveted prize long sought by civilized brigandage. To obtain possession of this vast wealth and reduce an intelligent people to the position of slaves, was by no means an easy task. But the promptings of avarice were not to be silenced, and greed was on the alert for an opportunity to seize the coveted prize. The fatal opportunity at last presented itself. African slavery had been a source of contention from the very foundation of the republic, and its agitation finally culminated in the secession of a majority of slave holding states. The war cloud was gathering and the mutterings of dissatisfaction were portentous of a coming storm. Old men ominously shook their heads ; young men stoutly declared that " the Union must be preserved "; and mothers on bended knee clasped more closely their precious boys, and prayed God that the storm cloud of war might pass. But above all the prayers, wailings and forebodings, the attentive listener could hear from Wall Street the echoes of jubilant satisfaction, and harmonious preparations for an onslaught upon the industry and prosperity of the country. Nor was Wall Street alone in this exultation over a prospective civil war ; all along the line were ringing notes of exultation, even our beloved Michigan swelled the cry " to arms !" led on by that great leader who startled the entire Christian world by his infamous declaration, " That a nation is not worth a curse without blood-letting." A declaration that must forever dishonor the name of its illustrious author.

Now do you ask why this exultation over a prospective civil war ? Do you ask why the money-kings of Wall Street and the great political chieftain of Michigan were so anxious, and positively joyous, when the guns were turned upon Fort Sumpter and the declaration of war sent its thrilling notes throughout the length and breadth of our land ? Do you ask why their hearts became like steel, and their thirst for human gore insatiable ? Why human life had lost its sacredness, and the thunderings of the war trumpet was music in their ears ? Reader, do you imagine it was because of their great love for the dusky toilers in the cotton fields of Mississippi, or because the finer instincts of their nature revolted against the cruel system of African slavery ? Do you suppose the story of Uncle Tom and Little Eva had touched their hearts and they had sworn vengeance upon the perpetrators of such cruelty ? No, no ; the money kings of Wall Street, and the great political chieftain of Michigan, were not the men whose hearts were touched with pity by the cries of distress. Their love of gain had stilled the finer instincts of their nature, and they rejoiced because they saw in the preparation for war their long-coveted opportunity for plunder. The calamity of war must bring its necessities, and through these necessities they determined to subjugate their unsuspecting brother men. To accomplish this it became necessary to obtain possession of the national finances. As blood, the circulating medium of the body, is the life of the body, so they knew that money, the circulating medium of the country, was the life of the country. Its industry, its education, its morality, in truth, its very life depended upon its medium of exchange. Controlling it, they could inflate or depress the business of the country at pleasure, they could send the warm life current through the channels of trade, dispensing peace, happiness and prosperity, or they could check its flow, and completely paralyze the industries of the country. They knew their opportunity was at hand, and the tidings of war that blanched the cheek and sent terror to the heart of the multitude was to their ears sweeter than the music of the spheres.

Scarcely had the war cloud broken ere the gold and silver money of the country disappeared. True to the history of metallic money in all ages, in the hour of peril, of a country's greatest need, her gold and silver money always takes flight. What had become of it ? Why Shylock had obtained possesion of it, for what purpose we shall see hereafter.

The necessities of the war required vast sums of money ; but the treasury was empty, the gold and silver money of the country had fled. What was to be done ? The government was in duty bound to suppress the rebellion, to defend herself against the aggressions of her enemy. She must call out troops, clothe, feed and provide them with munitions of war. She must equip hundreds of thousands of soldiers to to defend the liberties that had been entrusted to her keeping. But where should she derive means for this vast expenditure, where, in her distress, should she look for succor and support ? Where, indeed, could the government look except to her own moneyed classes ? Did not Wall Street rejoice in the declaration of war, and loudly protest against the secession of the slave States ? Surely, Wall Street would come to the rescue, and pour out her treasure in defense of the government. So said justice, so said patriotism, but history tells usquite another story. Neither American nor foreign capitalists would loan money to the government upon any reasonable terms. True the banks would loan their notes at 20 per cent. discount, that is, they would exchange eighty dollars of their notes for one hundred dollars in government bonds, bearing a high rate of interest, payable in gold, and backed by the government ; but they had not the power to make even these notes good in the hands of the soldier. Foreign capitalists would not at that time loan us any money, for they hoped and expected to see the republic rent in twain and the star of our liberty sink in a night of anarchy and blood.

Words are inadequate to express the hopeless condition of the country, and it would be almost impossible to give credence to the demands of avarice, were not its authenticity sustained by the most reliable records. From Appleton's Cyclopedia for 1861, page 296, we learn that the money kings of Wall Street graciously tendered loans to the government in her distress at from 24 to 36 per cent. interest—these same money kings whom today we hear quoted as those *generous, patriotic capitalists*. Why, sirs, the South itself was not more formidable and determined in the preservation of her slave property than were these Shylocks in their determination to wrench from the government in her distress, such usury as would have put to shame their world renowned ancestor. On the one hand appeared the bristling steel of the enemy ; on the other, disguised as a friend and urging on the war, stood Shylock clutching his gold and demanding therefor a rate of interest that would drain the life blood of the nation more effectually than the bullets of a Southern foe.

But what was Shylock to do ? The gold and silver of the country were in his possession, and they would not serve his purposes unless he could loan them to the government at exorbitant rates of interest. Knowing the necessities of the government these Shylocks determined to persist in their demands, for they had planned through the misfortune of the government to enrich and aggrandize themselves. This was why they rejoiced while others wept, this was why the tidings of war brought gladness to their hearts. By hoarding the gold and silver of the country they thought to *compel* the government to accede to their demands, and while the soldier was giving his life on the battle field they would gather to themselves riches and power.

But the great leader, Lincoln, was not to be baffled ; he loved the people better than Shylock, and justice better than oppression. From the constitution he read, " Congress shall have power to declare war." Again he read, " Congress shall have power to coin money." Then to the world he declared that Congress would coin money, and that the government, at whose head stood the fearless Lincoln, would *not* submit to the infamous demands of Shylock. Following this declaration came the enactments of July 17, 1861, and February 12, 1862, authorizing the issue of $60,000,000 treasury notes, not bearing interest and payable for all debts, public and private. These first issues of greenbacks constitute the demand notes, which, unlike all subsequent issues did *not contain the exception clause*, consequently they have always been at par with gold, and establish the fact, that had it not been for the exception clause on the greenback they would have always remained at par with gold. Wherever gold went these demand notes could go, even into the coffers of the bond-holders. They paid his interest, paid duties on imports, the millionaire took off his hat to them, and the banker made obeisance.

The issuance of this money at once brought relief to the country. With it the soldier was paid for his services, and his equipments furnished. Light began to break through the darkness that spread over the country, the destitution of the soldier's family gave way to moderate comfort, and although the pall of death was frequently spread at his door, its terror was relieved by the assurance that the government had made provision for his family. With an abundance of money, not even the blight of war could check the prosperity of the country, save in those sections desolated by its immediate ravages.

Commerce, industry and education received a new impetus, and flourished as never before in the history of the country.

But Shylock was sullen and disconsolate, having failed in his scheme to rob the people through exorbitant rates of interest, he immediately entered upon another scheme of brigandage which even the adroit Lincoln seemed unable to fathom. Having hoarded the gold and silver of the country, it was through this channel, if at all, he must despoil the country. Now, since Congress had made provision to supply the country with government money, there was no longer a demand for Shylock's hoarded gold, and his purposes seemed thwarted. But greed neither slumbers nor sleeps, nor did Shylock rest until his bandits had an appointed rendezvous. We find that only four days after the passage of the legal tender act to supply the country with government money, a bankers' convention was held in Washington, consisting of four delegates from New York banks, three from Philadelphia, and three from Boston. Shylock was alarmed ; he saw in the legal tender act a friend to the people, that it would transfer the monopoly of the money from his hands to the control of the people, he saw in it a precedent which, if established, would forever after enable the government to relieve itself and the people without submitting to his usurious extortions. He knew, too, that the government supplied with its own money would have no occasion to call from its hiding place his hoarded gold, unless by some means he could create a market for it. This, then, was plainly the object of that notable bankers' convention, *to create a demand far Shylock's hoarded gold.* Subsequent legislation tells us how well they succeeded.

CHAPTER II.
THE EXCEPTION CLAUSE.

To the busy world there was nothing remarkable in the calling of a convention at Washington. But why a *bankers'* convention ? And why called *immediately* upon the passage of the legal tender act ? What had been done that necessitated such a speedy gathering of the money mongers ? Why, Congress had made the money of the government full *legal tender for all debts*, and Shylock and his gold had been ignored. The bankers must have a consultation, and have it *at once*. They must get control of Congress and devise some means by which the demand for their gold would become imperative. There is left no room to doubt but that the conspiracy perfected at that convention resulted in that infamous exception clause on the greenback, and was consummated by act of Congress, February 25,1862, wherein it was stipulated that the greenback should be legal tender for all debts, public and private, *except duties on imports and interest on the public debt, which from that time forward should be paid in coin.* Shylock rejoiced ; he had accomplished his purpose, he had *created a demand for his gold.* Henceforth government should bow to him, and none should question his right to wield the golden scepter of money king. He had not conquered by bayonet or bowie knife, neither army nor navy had been at his command, but he had subjugated this people more effectually than ever Alexander or Napoleon had conquered.

For Congress to stipulate that only a certain article should be used in payment of certain government debts was simply to create a demand for that article. Had the act read that only white pigeons should be used in payment of interest and import duties, do you not see how a demand for white pigeons would have been created ? And if one hundred men had secured a corner on the pigeon business it would have been equivalent to a corner on the government. This is precisely what Congress did for Shylock—it gave him a corner on this government.

But I am asked what harm if Congress did create a demand for Shylock's hoarded gold ? The wage worker says it did not affect me, as I was working by the day, month or year. The manufacturer says it did not affect me, as I did not use imported material. The consumer says it made no difference with me, for I did not pay duties on imports, neither did I pay interest on bonds. Well, if none of these individuals were affected by this measure I am certainly in the wrong and most humbly beg your pardon, unless an investigation reveals a different state of affairs.

First we will see who paid the premium which Congress offered on Shylock's gold, and secondly how much Shylock was benefited thereby. You remember that during the war our cotton and sugar crops were cut off in the south and we were obliged to import these articles from foreign countries. At one time the duty on sugar was 76 per cent, about the same time the premium on gold was 185 per cent. That is, it took two hundred and eighty-five cents in greenbacks to buy one hundred cents in gold. Had it not been for the exception clause on the greenback the importer would have held his sugar at $1.76, but besides the import duty he must also pay the premium on the gold. One hundred cents in gold cost him two hundred and eighty-five cents in greenbacks. At the same rate, seventy-six (the import duty), cost him two hundred and sixteen cents in greenbacks, so that instead of paying 76 per cent duty he actually paid 216 per cent, or 140 per cent more than he would have paid had there been no exception clause on the greenback. This $1.40, which went directly into Shylock's coffers, was added to the price of the sugar and paid by the wage-worker, the manufacturer, and every other consumer of imported sugar. In the same way we were compelled to pay enormous prices for tea, coffee and several hundred imported articles. In the year 1864 the American people paid, in consequence of the exception clause, nearly four hundred million dollars, or about eighty-seven dollars to each family. With wages at $2.00 per day the head of each family worked forty-three and one-half days during the year, or nearly one day in each week for the gold gamblers of Wall Street. The government never received one farthing of that enormous sum, and the masses of the people never understood why they paid such exorbitant prices. Shylock did not go to them with bayonet and bowie-knife and *demand* their money, but in every pound of imported sugar, in every yard of imported clothing they paid him tribute just the same. The weapons with which he conquered were statutory laws enacted solely for his benefit. Think of the situation. The soldier facing death on the battle field for $16 per month, sends that money to his sorrow stricken family to be used in supplying them with the necessaries of life ; and in the purchase of their food and clothing with this blood-bought treasure, they pay indirectly to the gold gamblers of Wall Street from 25 to 50 per cent. Where is the man or the woman whose cheek does not burn with indignation and shame as he contemplates this robbery of the soldier and his family.

But again, the enormity of the crime did not end with Shylock's power to rob the people through import duties. The exception clause had depreciated the greenback. This was a part of Shylock's scheme. I know you have been told by the popular press and orators of every reason under heaven—except the right one—why the greenback was depreciated. They have told you it was because the Democrats cried them down ; and again, because so many were issued it was feared the government would not be able to redeem them. Why, my friends, if the best man in Michigan were to give his notes and then refuse to receive them for debts due himself could it have any other effect than to depreciate them ? I tell you it was a part of Shylock's scheme, nothing but depreciation could follow the exception clause. Now why did Shylock wish to depreciate the greenback ? Simply to enable him to get more of them in his possession with which to buy government bonds. Having purchased such legislation he could buy bonds with greenbacks at face value, and by means of the exception clause he could turn his gold into greenbacks at enormous advantage. Let us take a view of the situation.

It is A. D. 1864. The country is desolated by war. Scarcely a family in which death has not entered. Fathers, husbands, brothers and sons have been stricken down at the battle of Spottsylvania, or the Wilderness, and there is mourning throughout the land. The wail of the widow and the cry of fatherless children are heard alike in the homes of affluence and poverty. Mothers wring their hands and cry aloud in an agony of grief, an only son has been smitten down in the battle of the Wilderness, or perhaps a first-born, with shattered limbs, lies writhing and delirious in a distant hospital. The pall of death is over the land. But the clamor and clangor of business goes on.

A cargo of goods has entered one of our ports ; government requires the duty to be paid in gold. The importer proceeds at once to Wall Street, which, after the exception clause was placed on the greenback, became the great gold market of the earth, and as Judge Kelley justly said, " It invited from all the money centers of the world their most voracious vampires to come here and fatten upon the life-blood of the American people." Thither our importer wends his way, and as it chanced to be the month of July, 1864, he found he must pay $285 in legal tender money for $100 in gold. But there is no alternative, he pays the required sum, adds that much more to the price of his goods, and turns over the $100 in gold to the custom house officers, who duly deposit it in the United States Treasury. There we leave our importer, who has been compelled to add to the price of his goods, not only the import duty but also the enormous premium on Shylock's gold. Let us now return to our Wall Street broker and see how he has been effected by the calamity of war. The $285 in greenbacks, which the importer paid him for the $100 in gold, he immediately invests in government bonds at face value. His next step is to draw interest on his bonds, for the act of February 25, 1862, stipulated that his interest should not only be paid in *gold* but in *advance*. Having drawn his gold interest in advance he is prepared on the morrow to sell it to the next importer, and with each exchange he clears $185 on every $100 in gold. Shall we ever cease to extol the patriotism of those Wall Street capitalists ? But our picture is not complete until we take a look at the soldier. Sixteen dollars per month seems a small compensation for one to stand before death in its multitude of forms. But the soldier's love of country overcame his fear of death, and he braved the terrors of the battle field that he might bequeath to his little ones the inheritance of liberty ; and if not impelled by love of country, the government did not hesitate to use its prerogative of " drafting into the service." But did it draft money ? No. It must not interfere with the " sacred rights of property." Human life must be sacrificed for its protection, but property was inviolable.

During the latter part of the war the government paid the soldier $16 per month in greenbacks for risking his life on the battle field ; with this he could purchase just $16 in government bonds. But the government paid Shylock in gold for risking his credit, and for sixteen dollars in gold, during the month of July 1864, he could purchase $43.60 in government bonds. The question now arises, how much did the government actually pay the soldier, and how much is still due him ? Morally, and I believe legally, our government is today under greater financial obligations to the soldier than it is to the bond holder. Who will dare to say that human life is less sacred than capital ? Or that every greenback dollar paid the soldier was not redeemed by his service—perhaps his life ? Is there a quality in redemption that asks a higher price than agony and blood ?

President Cleveland has been greatly censured for vetoing private pension bills, but how many of those who condemn him uphold the action of the government that perpetrated this wholesale robbery upon the soldier ? And how many of them voted against General Weaver's bill for making up to the soldiers the difference between gold and the depreciated currency in which they were paid ? It is folly to claim that the war and business could not have been carried on without Shylock's gold. We have already shown that the government after issuing its own money—the greenback—had no need of gold, until, through strategy, the exception clause was placed on the greenback, and placed there for no other purpose than that of creating a demand for the gold hoarded by the money kings of the country.

During the past few years, several states have made large appropriations for the erection of soldiers' homes. Doubtless to many this seems a very beneficent act on the part of the government, but is it beneficence when the robber restores a part of his ill-gotten gains to the man he has victimized ? Had the interests of the soldier been as carefully guarded during the war as were the interests of the money monger, there is no doubt but that many who today languish in these institutions would be comfortable and happy in homes of their own, independent of either public or private charity.

CHAPTER III.
NATIONAL BANKING SYSTEM.

THE next scheme for robbing the people was the national bank act, passed in 1863. Of all the villainous schemes of robbery ever practiced upon any people our national banking system stands preeminent. By it Shylock was permitted to invest his greenbacks in government bonds at face value ; upon these bonds he not only drew gold interest in advance but by means of the bank scheme he actually had 90 per cent of their value returned to him. While drawing interest upon the entire investment in the form of bonds, 90 per cent of it has been returned to him in the form of national bank notes, and it is with these he carries on his banking business, loaning them out upon the most advantageous terms. On the one hand he draws interest from the government ; on the other, *from the same investment* he draws interest from his individual debtors.

For instance, you borrow $100 from your national banker, he graciously loans it to you at ten per cent in advance, which actually leaves you but $90. With this $90 you supply your family with food and clothing, upon a large part of which, as we have already shown, you pay an import duty, this import duty, please remember, went into the treasury and from thence paid interest on this same banker's bonds. Now is it not clear that your banker has been paid two interests upon the same money, one directly upon the bank notes, presented him by the government, which he loaned to you at ten per cent interest, the other indirectly as interest on his bonds, which was paid with the import duty that had been added to the price of your goods ? Now it is not for me to condemn individuals for taking advantage of this infamous law, but we do in most unqualified terms, denounce such a system of public robbery. None but the wealthy classes are able to enter upon this profitable banking business. If it is proper for the government to make the business of the wealthy thus lucrative, is it not equally just to give like advantages to the poorer classes ?

A wise government will look to the interests of its wealth producers who constitute the great toiling masses, and a just government would make the way to prosperity as easy for its humblest as for its most wealthy citizen. If this system is good for banking it ought to be good for every other legitimate enterprise, and every other law-abiding citizen is entitled to like consideration.

Let us see how this system would affect, that great industrial class, the farmer. To illustrate : Mr. Jones is a farmer in easy circumstances ; the markets are favorable and he concludes to sell his wheat crop ; accordingly he hauls 1,000 bushels to market ; having no immediate use for the money, he agrees with the buyer to sell at $1 per bushel and take in payment this $1,000 note. It is a long-time note, fully secured, bears a good rate of interest, payable in gold semi-annually in advance. Mr. Jones being well secured, feels that he has made a good exchange, in place of property idle and subject to loss in his granary, it is now safe and yielding a handsome income. He is congratulating himself upon his ability as a financier, when he is accosted by the dealer, who informs him that he —the dealer—has on hand another variety of wheat equally good as that he had just purchased, and since he had found Mr. Jones a keen, thrifty business man, he would present him with 900 bushels of it. The only expense to Mr. Jones would be the cost of handling, which would be one per cent of the value of the wheat, or $9. The wheat should be taken to Mr. Jones' granary, where he could loan it to his neighbors upon the most advantageous terms. Nothing would be required of him for twenty years ; at the end of that time, unless they could enter into a new contract, it would be necessary for him to return the 900 bushels of wheat ; nothing would be required of him for the use of it, although by judiciously loaning to his neighbors twenty fold had been returned to him.

Words could scarcely express the surprise of Mr. Jones upon hearing this irrational proposition. We may imagine him taking the $1,000 note from his pocket, and scrutinizing it with the gravest suspicions, or inspecting the shining gold pieces—his advance interest—to satisfy himself that they are not spurious. But being reassured, he hastens home to carry the news of his good fortune to the partner of his joys. He playfully drops the shining gold pieces into her lap, with the assurance that they are partial proceeds of the wheat, and that they are hers to invest in the new silk she had so long desired. Mrs. Jones expresses great surprise, for she had been previously informed that a $1,000 interest bearing note would be the return for the wheat. Mr. Jones complacently taking the note from his pocket, informs her that the gold pieces are simply the *advance* interest on his note ; he then expatiates upon the beauties and advantages of such a system, declaring that hereafter his notes must be drawn with interest payable in advance. Then with an air of haughty indifference, he informs her that besides the gold interest and $1,000 note, 900 bushels of wheat were being returned to him, and that the very men who hauled away the 1,000 bushels in the morning were returning with 900 to be replaced in his granary.

This announcement was too startling for truth-loving Mrs. Jones. She threw up her hands in horror ; for twenty-eight years she had been the wife of Darius Jones, and for the first time in all these years she had occasion to doubt his veracity. But the unwelcome thought was checked as a shudder of fear ran through her frame. " Poor Darius," thought she, " must be insane." Great sobs of grief began to choke her utterance, when casually glancing out of the window, she saw a train of loaded wagons coming up the lane. She stood for a moment dazed, great beads of perspiration appeared on her forhead. She looked at Darius, at the approaching train, then nervously scanning the $1,000 note, she pushed it with the gold from her, and burst into a flood of agonizing tears. It was long before Darius could reconcile his wife to this mysterious proceeding, but there was a vein of ambition in her nature which dominated at times, and when she saw the benefits that must accrue from such a transaction, she not only became reconciled but regarded with pride the acumen that had so increased their material prosperity. From that time the Joneses moved in the most aristocratic circles, and were accounted among the "best" people of the community.

To many of my readers, no doubt, this little story appears like a most exaggerated fiction, but truth is stranger than fiction, and this truth is not only strange but startling. He who doubts its authenticity has only to read the laws which govern our national banking institutions, and in proof of the rapacity of the system let me add that there is today a bill pending in congress, whereby it is proposed to make the bank circulation, not 90 but 100 per cent, the full face value of the bond ; in other words, Mr. Jones proposes the return of a full 1,000 bushels of wheat in addition to his $1,000 bond and advanced gold interest. But the clear-headed, vigilant Weaver is on guard, and to him the people may safely entrust this momentous question. Further, the national banks, as depositories for the U.S. Treasury, today hold $59,000,000 of the people's money upon which they are not paying one cent interest, but are and have been for the last 20 years loaning it at from 8 to 10 per cent, or using it for effecting corners on the necessaries of life. At one time the First National Bank of New York—John Sherman's bank—had the free use of $43,000,000 of the people's money, at a time when its own capital stock was less than a quarter of a million. It was thus that *honest* John Sherman "east anchor to windward" when he was the people's servant.

The founders of our government had a salutary dread of the bankers' influence making itself felt in shaping the national legislation. They anticipated the evils that we have seen in our days to result from allowing the banking interest to become dominant in the halls of Congress. We find, therefore, the Third Congress of the United States Senate passing the following resolution on the 23d of December, 1793:

> " Any person holding *any office or any stock* in any institution *in the nature of a bank* for issuing or discounting bills or notes payable to bearer or order, *cannot be a member of the House whilst he holds such office or stock.*"

The resolution was signed by the President, George Washington.

At that time there were only three banks in the whole country. Yet even then Congress thought that the bank influence was such a standing danger to the maintenance of legislative purity that it deemed it necessary to provide against it by special legislation.

The three banks of 1793 have grown to over 3,000, and the banking interest as we have seen at one time had 189 representatives in Congress, the next largest representation being that of the legal profession, while the industrial classes were comparatively without any representation.

It is hardly necessary to point out the results of the large preponderance of bankers in Congress. It has for years been seen in the whole tenor of Congressional legislation. The interests of the industrial classes have been constantly and systematically sacrificed, while the interests of the moneyed classes have been persistently pushed to the front. Now has the law of 1793 been repealed ? If not, are there not enough honest men in Congress to see that it is put into effect ? Unless something be speedily done to revive this law, our government will soon be openly, as it already is secretly, a bankers' government.

If anyone doubts that the national banking system was not deliberately planned for the purpose of robbing the people, he may be undeceived by a careful perusal of the following private circular, sent out to the bankers of the country by their secretary, James Buell. Here is the circular :

DEAR SIR—It is advisable to do all in your power to sustain such daily and prominent weekly newspapers, especially the agricultural and religious press, as will oppose the issuing of greenback paper money, and that you withhold patronage or favors from all applicants who are not willing to oppose the government issue of money. Let the government issue the coin and the banks issue the paper money of the country, for then we can better protect each other. To repeal the law creating national banks, or to restore to circulation the government issue of money, will be to provide the people with money, and will therefore seriously affect your individual profits as banker and lender. See your member of Congress at once, and engage him to support our interest, that we may control legislation.

(Signed by the Secretary.)
JAS. BUEL,
No. 147 Broadway (Room 4), New York.

Mark you it is especially *the agricultural and religious press* through which the secretary designs working upon the prejudices of the people. Surely not a very tame reflection upon the intelligence of these classes, but when we hear the so-called Christian minister upholding such a system of class legislation, it is evident that at least so far as such religionists are concerned, Mr. Buell did not " reckon without his host."

Now we have no more right to condemn the men who have taken advantage of our banking laws than we have to condemn the liquor seller who complies with the requirements of the liquor law. They are both law-abiding citizens, both doing a legitimate business. The trouble is not with the individuals, but with the law. Comparatively few men will be better than the law makes them. So long as robbery is legalized, we must be afflicted with robbers. This morning the country is horrified with the news of a shocking railroad disaster, and the horror is magnified by the rumor that ghouls in human form perpetrated the most fiendish robberies upon the dead and dying ; indeed it is even asserted that these fiends planned the disaster for the sole purpose of robbing the victims. But we have another picture. The life of our nation is trembling in the balance. A million of armed men face each other on the battlefield, the roar of artillery and the thunderous note of the cannon send desolation to thousands of stricken households ; our country is one vast graveyard, and the land is red with fratricidal blood. In our nation's capitol are assembled the law makers of the land ; among them are those who encouraged and urged on the war, who declared that " a nation is not worth a curse without blood-letting." These are they who sat in our congressional halls and speculated upon the most effectual means of robbing the widows and orphans of these dead and dying soldiers, who instituted laws by which the children and children's children of these helpless soldiers should henceforth become their wage-slaves, and the bondmen of their children through all generations. Laws which, unless repealed, are destined soon to crush out the liberties of the people and the life of our Republic. Theirs was legalized robbery—the railroad bandits wrecked only a train—but these a nation.

CHAPTER IV.
CONTRACTION.

THE third scheme of robbery was that of *contracting the currency* by destroying the greenbacks. In pursuance of this plan the act of April 12, 1866, was passed whereby it was provided that a regular and systematic cremation of greenbacks should take place.

Let it be remembered that upon this government money the greenback, the people did not pay interest. It was backed by the government, which made it safe and reliable, and issued in sums convenient for small as well as large business transactions. The money monger, with $1,000 in greenbacks, had found it necessary to employ that money in order to derive any profit from it. This added to his care, which apparently was the very thing he sought to avoid ; investments in commerce and manufacturing required his personal supervision ; investments in houses and land incurred taxation, risks, and often loss ; but investment in bonds seemed quite suited to his esthetical tastes, for they returned a rich golden harvest, without any of the annoyances of taxation, insurance or even the care of looking after his investments.

Is it any wonder he hailed with joy the contraction policy, and gladly gave his $1,000 in greenbacks (to be consigned to the furnace), in exchange for a $1,000 untaxed, interest-bearing bond ? But what of labor seeking employment ? Shylock has invested his property in bonds, he has no need of labor ; true, labor must pay the interest on his bonds, but he has no employment for it. While this $1,000 was in government money it could have given two men employment in some profitable business ; but with his money invested in bonds, he kicks labor into the street and growls about the inefficiency of the tramp law. He does nothing whatever to advance the interests of labor, but drains its life-blood in payment of his everlasting interest. By investing the $1,000 in bonds it is taken from circulation. There is $1,000 less for the people to do business with, and $1,000 more for them to pay interest upon.

Again, by contracting the volume of money it lowered the prices of other property and added that much more to the burdens of the debtor class. For instance, Mr. Burt bought a farm for $6,000, when wheat was $2 per bushel. He paid $3,000 cash, and placed upon it a mortgage for the remaining $3,000, which he expected to pay with wheat at $2 per bushel. A part of the $3,000 cash invested in the farm was Mr. Burt's savings from his services in the army. He was a good soldier and bore testimony of having seen active service. He was one of the first to enlist, and stood by the old flag until the last shot was fired, then he returned home, determined to spend the remainder of his days in the enjoyment of that peace so nobly won ; accordingly he purchased his farm, little dreaming of the vicissitudes that awaited him.

Before the first pay day came the money of the country had been contracted 25 per cent, the price of wheat had been reduced in the same ratio, from $2.00 to $1.50 per bushel. Neither the debt nor interest had in any way been contracted, and Mr. B. found it necessary to hire $250 to make up his payment. He had not been disappointed in his wheat crop, it was even better than he expected, but for some inexplicable reason the *price* was not what he expected. He was told there had been an over-production of wheat, that the supply was greater than the demand ; and yet he knew that one of his neighbors, a day laborer, had never been so hard pushed to keep the wolf from the door. The laborer was sober and industrious, Mr. Burt had often employed him ; but since the price of wheat had declined, he must economize, and the first step in economy was to reduce the wages of his "help."

When the next payment came due, wheat brought but $1 per bushel, and Mr. Burt was obliged to hire $500 to meet his payment. In applying to a national banker for assistance, he found that "money was scarce, but he would try and get it for him at one per cent a month." Mr. Burt concluded to look farther, and after a long search found a "friend" who decided to let him have the amount at 10 per cent in *advance*. This, taken from the $500, left him $450. The other $50 was made up by selling a few sheep and the best cow. Heretofore the butter had furnished Mrs. B. the means for keeping the children respectably clothed, but now the cow had gone and there was no means of replenishing their clothing. Susan, John, Willie and even little Mary, were extremely sensitive, and when their clothes began to be shabby their fondness for the Sunday school declined. Mr. Burt did not renew his church subscription that year, and it was very uncomfortable for him to sit in his pew and hear the minister preach about the worldly minded man, who thought more about the price of wheat than of his soul's Salvation, and who grew so avaricious that he would not subscribe for the support of the gospel. Mr. Burt listened to what the preacher said, but his heart grew hard, his clothes grew shabby, and his attendance at church grew infrequent and finally ceased altogether.

A few weeks before the third and final payment came due, Mr. Burt sold his wheat at 75 cents per bushel ; a fine crop, but it failed to meet the requirements of the contract, foreclosure followed, and Mr. Burt and family were turned penniless into the street. Setting out in search of work he unfortunately reached Michigan just after her tramp law had taken effect. Wandering from place to place, shabbily dressed and "without any visible means of support," he was finally arrested for vagrancy, and sent to the penitentiary. Disheartened and overcome by a feeling of disgrace, he soon sickened and died. His friends, ignorant of his whereabouts, knew nothing of his sad fate. Twenty-four hours after his death, on a bleak December day, a rough wooden box was landed at the basement window of the medical department of the Athens of Michigan, and a few days later a subject with care-worn look and locks prematurely grey, was laid upon the dissecting table. The students jocosely remarked that "the old fellow must have been a soldier, judging from the number of scars upon his person." But there was one student who did not join in the merriment of his companions. He earnestly scanned the features of the dead man, and half an hour after the dismissal of the class a missive was winging its way to the state penitentiary. The next day the expressman brought a little package to the serious student. He opened it with trembling hands ; alas, his conjectures were realities. The package contained a few articles of clothing, and in a little soiled packet he found some mementoes from his father's house, among them the picture of a beautiful maiden, his sister Mary, and by her side a young man in soldier's uniform. The blood curdled in his veins. He remembered when that picture was taken, though only a child ; the occasion was indelibly fixed upon his mind. It was the day that his sister was married to the soldier—Joseph Burt—the pauper of yesterday, the victim of the dissecting knife. Spared from the shot and shell of the battlefield to die a pauper's death, and to suffer a fate that none but criminals should ever know. Ah, my country ! where is thy gratitude ?

Through the contraction of the currency Mr. Burt's debt was doubled, and what is true of this unfortunate debt is equally true of the debt of the government. Notwithstanding John Sherman said to the laboring people of Ohio less than a year ago that "the debt is nearly paid off," yet it is a fact that this debt is a greater burden upon us today than it was at the close of the war. That is, our debt-paying power has been reduced in a far greater ratio than the debt itself, and today it would take more bushels of wheat, more tons of hay, or more bales of cotton, to pay our national debt than it would have taken at the close of the war. What is true of the debt is equally true of the interest, and notwithstanding we have paid interest enough to have twice paid the original debt, it will take more pounds of beef, pork, or wool, more day's labor to pay our interest this year than it took in 1866. The effects of contraction on the morals of the country is briefly depicted by a Georgia editor as follows :

> In 1868 there was about $40 per capita of money in circulation ; cotton was about 30 cents a pound. The farmer then put a 500 pound bale of cotton on his wagon, took it to town and sold it. Then he paid $40 taxes, bought a cooking stove for $30, a suit of clothes for $15, his wife a dress for $5, 100 pounds of meat for $18, 1 barrel of flour for $12, and went home with $30 in his pocket. In 1887 there was about $5 per capita of money in circulation ; this same farmer put a 500 pound bale of cotton on his wagon, went to town and sold it, paid $40 taxes, got discouraged, went to the saloon, spent his remaining $2.30 and went home dead broke and drunk.

There is no doubt but it was the avowed policy of the party in power to retire from circulation and utterly destroy every dollar of greenback currency. Words are inadequate to express the horror that such a movement would have precipitated upon the people. It is enough to know the results of ten years of such legislation. Ten years in which our government circulation was reduced nearly fourteen hundred million dollars, and swept into the vortex of financial ruin thousands and tens of thousands of our grandest and truest men. In the words of a philanthropic journalist we will review the history of the ten years of contraction :

> On the 12th day of April, 1866, congress passed a law authorizing the secretary of the treasury to sell 5-20 bonds, and with the proceeds *retire United States currency, including greenbacks.*
> On Dec. 4, 1866, E.G. Spalding, a Buffalo, N.Y., banker, a member of congress, wrote to Secretary McCulloch as follows :
> You, no doubt, now, to a certain extent, *have control of the currency of the country,* and I think that you will, of necessity, *contract moderately,* so

as to preserve a *tolerable easy money market*. There may be *occasional spasms or tightness* for money, but generally, I shall look for plenty of money, for *at least one year to come*.

When this letter was written the country was in possession of $1,996,687,770 currency.

During this year, there were but 520 business failures in the whole country, involving a loss of but $17,625,000.

Labor was well paid and fully employed.

1867.

This year the work of contraction was vigorously pushed, and there were 2,386 failures, with a total loss of $86,218,000.

1868.

During this year, $473,000,000 of money was destroyed, and failures increased to 2,608, with a loss to creditors of $63,774,000. Money began to be tight, and financial "spasms" were frequent.

1869.

During this year over $500,000,000 of money passed into the cremation furnace, producing 2,799 business failures, and a loss of $75,054,900. Money growing tighter and wages lower.

1870.

This year $67,000,000 of money was destroyed, and 3,551 failures took place, involving a loss of $88,242,000. Money very scarce and wages of labor were reduced all over the country.

1871.

Thirty-five millions of money this year is retired, with 2,915 failures and a loss of $85,250,000. More men out of work and wages cut down.

1872.

Only about $12,000,000 was destroyed this year, but such had been the strain upon the business of the country for the past five years that this proved the last straw to 4,069 business firms, involving a loss of $121,058,000. More cutting of wages and strikes talked of.

1873.

This year the storm reached its climax. Business had hoped that, with every returning season, prospects would brighten and money would become plenty. Instead of this, however, notwithstanding but $1,609,000 were destroyed, the people became panic-stricken, and 5,183 business firms were precipitated, with a loss of $228,499,000. Five hundred thousand men are thrown out of employment, wages cut down all over the country, and strikes are of frequent occurrence.

1874.

Notwithstanding the terrible results of the last year, the wine-press of contraction still creaks on its hinges of death, as round and round it sweeps out of circulation $75.484,000 certificates of indebtedness, which have been made legal tender money, $85,760,000 treasury notes, $6,335,045 legal tenders, $3,000,000 fractional currency, and $1,000,000 bank notes, producing 5,832 failures, and a loss of $155,239,000 to creditors. A million idle men began to tramp in search of work. Wages still decline and strikes more numerous.

1875.

The volume of currency, this year, was contracted $40,817,418 and the failures reach 7,740, with loss to creditors of $201,060,000. Two millions of laborers out of work. Famine and hunger begin to stare them in the face, and "tramping" becomes a profession.

1876.

According to the most reliable estimates, the contraction of the currency this year, in the destruction of greenbacks, and the withdrawal of bank currency amounts to about $85,000,000, with 9,092 failures, and $191,000,000 loss, during the *first quarter of the year*. The aggregate failures of the year reached over 10,000, with losses not less than $300,000,000. This does not include losses to stockholders, by foreclosure and sale of railroads.

What a record for ten years ! Who wonders times were hard, and men idle ? Still with all this array of wreck and ruin, with the finger-board of contraction at the close of each year, pointing to the cause, the people were asleep, or on their knees praying for some interposition of Providence in their behalf, while John Sherman went marching on with the torch of death, to burn the remaining $300,000,000 of the the people's money.

Three million men are out of employment.

Bankruptcies multiplying with great rapidity.

The tramp nuisance culminates.

Wages are cut down to starvation prices.

Strikes, riots and general consternation seize the people, and the circulation is cut down to $606,000,000.

1877.

The red torch of the vandal lighted up the country from Pittsburg to Chicago. These are the footprints of the red-mouthed despots, the money power, which is still forging chains for the limbs of American industry, with a view to enslaving the American populace by robbing them of their homes and firesides, and thus controling their life, liberty, and pursuits of happiness by controling their wages through the control and monopoly of money.

These are God's truths which the people can heed and be saved, or heed not and the Republic be lost.

CHAPTER V.
CREDIT-STRENGTHENING ACT.

BUT we have not yet completed the enumeration of crimes perpetrated against the people of this country through this infernal system of legalized robbery. Having purchased their bonds with government money, depreciated from 38 to 60 per cent (on account of the exception clause) and having exempted them from taxation, with advanced interest payable in gold, it would seem that the climax of audacity had been reached. But who can fathom the greed of the money shark, or set bounds to the voracity of a civilized brigand

The fourth act in Shylock's tragedy, by which the government and this great people were sacrificed, is familiarly known as the *credit-strengthening act*, by which the 5-20 bonds were made payable in coin. This act, approved March 18, 1869, added to the burdens of the people more than six hundred millions of dollars. It is claimed by many bond holders and their leaders, that the act which authorized the issue of these bonds made them payable in gold. But there is no such possible interpretation of the act, and if they were issued payable in gold in the first place why did they pass the credit strengthening act of 1869 ? The very fact that they passed that act four years after the close of the war, when the country was at peace with the world and itself, is proof beyond question that they were at first made payable in legal tender, and that this law was passed for no other purpose than that of doubling the wealth of the bond holder, which, of necessity, must and *did* double the burdens of the people. Further, we have undeniable proof that the act was secured through the most soulless strategy, and that Grant, Sherman and Morton were parties to it. There is not the slightest doubt but that Grant's election to the presidency, and Sherman's appointment to the treasury were secured through their pledges to obtain the passage of this infamous act. Those who opposed the measure were denounced as repudiators, and in his inaugural address Grant warned his party that no repudiator of one farthing of the public debt would be trusted in public place. Immediately upon his inauguration an extra session of Congress was called. The first bill presented, the first bill passed, the first act approved, the first document sighed by President Grant was this infamous credit-strengthening act, by which the people who placed him in power, were robbed of millions of dollars. Circumstantial evidence also proves beyond doubt that the election of Grant and the defeat of Seymour was a bargain and sale between the leaders of the old parties, and the most villainous betrayal of public trust ever practiced upon an unsuspecting people. There had been an attempt to pass the credit-strengthening act during the session of 1867 and 1868 but it failed. During its pending, a presidential nomination and election took place. The Democratic party nominated Horatio Seymour on a platform opposed to the coin payment of currency obligations. The Republican party nominated U.S. Grant on the urgent solicitation and petition of forty capitalists of New York City.

August Belmont was chairman of the Democratic national committee ; he was also agent of the Rothschilds, who were in possession of several hundred millions of the 5-20 bonds, and particularly interested in the credit-strengthening act. As early as March 13, 1868, Baron James Rothschild instructed August Belmont that unless the Democratic party went in for paying the 5-20 bonds in gold it *must be defeated.* The first step was to have the convention held in New York City, and it convened July 4, 1868. Belmont was unable to control the convention, or at least that part of the platform pertaining to the coin payment of bonds. But besides being chairman of the Democratic national committee, he also owned a large interest in the New York *World*, the leading Democratic paper in the country. Although he had made a sale (doubtless a sham) of his interest in the paper, he could still control it more easily than he could control the Democratic convention, and on the 15th of October, only a few days before election, it came out with a double-leaded editorial denouncing Seymour as unavailable and unfit for president and advised his withdrawal.

This action had the effect for which undoubtedly it was intended, that of demoralizing the Democratic party on the eve of election, thus insuring the election of Grant, who had pledged himself to the money power. During the previous session of Congress, Oliver P. Morton made a speech in which he said :

> We would do foul injustice to the government and to the people of the United States after we have sold these bonds, on an average of not more than sixty cents on the dollar, now to propose to make a new contract for the benefit of the bond holder.

Hon. Thad. Stevens, in speaking of the insatiate demands of the money bond-interest said :

> We were foolish enough to grant them gold interest, and now they unblushingly demand further advantages ; the truth is, we can never satisfy their appetite for money.

And on his death bed, said :

> Yes, we had to yield. The Senate was stubborn. We did not, however, until we found the country must be lost or the bankers gratified. And we have sought to save the country in spite of the cupidity of its wealthier citizens.

Ben Wade, of Ohio, in a letter written at Washington, Dec. 13, 1867, expressed himself as follows :

> I am for the laboring portion of our people, the rich will take care of themselves. * * * * We never agreed to pay the five-twenties in gold ; no man can find it in the bond, and I will never consent to have one payment for the bond holder and another for the people. It will sink any party and it ought to.

In regard to this policy, John Sherman, in a speech delivered Feb. 27, 1867, said :

> *I say that equality and justice are amply satisfied if we redeem these bonds at the end of five years in the same kind of money, of the same intrinsic value it bore at the time they were issued.* Gentlemen may reason about this matter over and over again, and they cannot come to any other conclusion at least that has been my conclusion after the most careful consideration. Senators are sometimes in the habit, in order to defeat the argument of an antagonist, of saying that this is repudiation. Why, sirs, every citizen of the United States has conformed his business to the legal tender clause. He has collected and paid his debts accordingly.

And in a letter dated Feb. 20, 1868, he said :

> Your idea that we propose to violate or repudiate a promise when we offer to redeem the principal in legal tenders is erroneous. I think the bond holder violates his promise when he refuses to take the same kind of money he paid for the bonds.
> The bond holder can demand only the kind of money he paid, and he is *a repudiator* and *extortioner* to demand money more valuable than he gave.

John Sherman, at that time, was comparatively a poor man and, no doubt, an honest man ; his appetite for pelf had not been awakened, or at least, to that degree which permitted him to sacrifice honor in its getting.

In 1875 John Sherman said, " We are following in the footsteps of England," and no one knew better than he the scheme that had brought us to that deplorable condition. In 1879 this same John Sherman, then a millionaire, in a speech made in Toledo, said that " To *refuse* to pay the bonds in gold would be repudiation and extortion, and would be scoffing at the blessings of Almighty God." Think of it ! A man becoming a millionaire out of a $5,000 salary, and then talk as if he had anything to do with Almighty God. But as John Sherman grew rich, the country grew poor ; merchants were driven to bankruptcy, farmers were driven into debt, and finally off their farms. Workmen were driven out of employment, and tramps thronged the highways. Despair and ruin sat enthroned in the hearts and homes of this great people.

The above let it be remembered, is testimony from leading Republicans of that time, but who, upon the election of Grant to the presidency, either sealed their lips upon this subject or, like Sherman, openly and shamelessly advocated the abominable swindle.

Here let me add, that when the bill passed, legalizing this gigantic robbery, there were 189 bankers, and many bond holders in the two houses, while as lobbyists and agents of the heavy bond holders there was an army of workers and feed attorneys, all working for the passage of that atrocious bill, while honest industry was powerless in self-defence. One shudders to think of these vandals in the temple of our liberty. They desecrated the sanctuary of our fathers, and despoiled the heritage of their children.

The blood curdles to think of Washington and that fratricidal conspirator at the head of the same government.

CHAPTER VI.
REFUNDING.

THE next and fifth step in the infernal scheme was that of refunding the national debt. Few people ever comprehended the enormity of that crime, and never was there a deeper laid plot to reduce a people to abject and hopeless servitude.

This act, approved July 14, 1870, provided for the refunding of the national debt. In other words, it was a scheme to perpetuate the debt and a plot against the people to keep them forever under the yoke of bondage. Webster's definition of the funding system fully expresses the design of Congress in passing this act ; he says : To fund—to put into the form of bonds or stocks bearing annual interest. To refund is to renew these bonds or stocks, perhaps under a new contract, which changes the rate of interest, though the interest continues. Funding system is "a scheme of finance or revenue by which provision is made for paying annual interest on a public debt." Mark you, it is a *scheme*, and no provision is made for paying the debt itself. The refunding of this bonded, untaxed, interest-bearing debt is a calamity upon this people, for it has placed the burden beyond the control of the generation that created it ; we have already paid interest enough to have twice paid the debt, and yet today it is a greater burden upon the people than it was at the close of the war.

The evil effects of this system are at this time especially apparent. With money enough in the treasury today half the public debt, the people are debarred this privilege, because the villainous act of refunding has postponed the time of payment from ten to twenty years. In consequence of this nefarious act, about $750,000,000 of the debt cannot be paid until 1907.

Consequently, with an enormous sum of money lying idle in the treasury (or what is still more intolerable, deposited with national banks which have been granted its free use for more than twenty years) the people are not only deprived of its use in their business, but are still compelled to pay interest upon the entire amount.

Now, would you have any confidence in the business ability of a man who would so arrange a large indebtedness that he should continue to pay interest upon the entire debt after he had accumulated the means for liquidating a large part of it ? And yet this is the very policy embodied in the funding act of 1870. And further, the same party that enacted this law is today putting forth every effort for the expenditure of this surplus, in any and every other way then that of liquidating the national debt. The Direct Tax bill, the Educational bill, the River and Harbor bills, the Pension bills, bills to provide for coast defences, and other innumerable bills for disposing of the surplus are, in the main, schemes concocted for the sole purpose of using this surplus in such a way as to prevent the payment of the bonds and to continue the infernal system of taxation which is wringing the life blood from the people, and which affords the only plausible pretext for maintaining party lines between the two old organizations.

But this is not all ; during the present session of Congress, the indomitable Weaver has made the startling discovery that this funding bill never passed Congress in the form in which it appears upon the statute books. By the changing of a single word the import of the entire bill was so changed as to make the four per cent bonds payable only *after* thirty years, instead of previous to that time. The anarchism of 1887, under its worst construction, sinks into insignificance before the light of such diabolical assassination of law.

The object of funding our debt was to establish a bond system on the same plan of England's bonded debt. England's debt, which commenced with the same infamous banking system which we have adopted, was established two centuries ago. The interest on her debts supports a few idle aristocrats, but it has reduced to ignorance and degradation millions of her toiling people. Another object of funding our debt was to build up a moneyed oligarchy, and an aristocracy of wealth to compete with that of our ancient foe.

That those who have long controlled our government are determined to carry out their plan does not admit the slighest doubt. The bill of Congressman White, now pending, to refund the entire national debt into a fifty-year 2½ per cent bond, also the bill of Senator Farwell to perpetuate the national banks, adds to the evidences of their determination to saddle this interminable burden upon the American people.

There is but one interpretation to the funding act ; its object is to compel our children and children's children, through all generations, to serve the children of these bond holders. Voter, is this the legacy you intended to bequeath to your children ? Is this the liberty they are to thank their fathers for ? Born slaves to aristocrats ! And yet this is the inheritance the money king would bequeath to the posterity of labor in America ; this is what the old parties are asking you to do ; this is what for twenty-five years you have been doing, bartering away this blood-bought inheritance, selling the birth-rights of your children. And what have you received in return ? Mortgaged homes, endless taxes, unremitting and unrequited toil. Is this any better than the inheritance of slaves ? And will you permit this bondage to continue ? Are the ties of party so dear that liberty, home and family must be sacrificed upon its altar ? In the name of your homes and the children that bless them ; in the name of thousands of homes, and tens of thousands of wrecked and ruined lives I entreat you to break this party thralldom and smite down this iniquitous legislation.

CHAPTER VII.
DEMONETIZATION OF SILVER.

HAVING refunded and made payable in coin the bonds which had not cost their holders more than sixty cents on the dollar, the casual observer is satisfied that the last robbery has been perpetrated. But the busy brain of avarice is ever reaching out, not after new truths, but for gain, *gain*, GAIN ; and we next find these civilized brigands have consummated a scheme for the *demonetization of silver*. This act, passed, in 1873, destroyed the money quality of silver, and thus produced a farther contraction of the currency. The object of this act was first to prevent the payment of the bonds, and second to increase their value.

Never in this country had there been an investment so safe and yet so reliable. Shylock, with his hoarded millions, could rest on beds of down. Neither fire, flood, mildew nor blight brought anxiety to him. He seemed to rest in assurance of the Divine favor, having obeyed the injunction to "lay up his treasure where moth and rust could not corrupt, nor thieves break through and steal." Indeed, the entire country had become sponsor for his wealth, for under the law every producer and millions of wage-workers had been instituted a vigilance committee to look after his welfare. Why should he not be opposed to having his bond investment disturbed ? The government held that property in safe keeping and did not charge a cent for the favor ; it collected his interest and paid it over to him free of charge ; it paid his gold interest in advance and exempted him from taxation ; the insurance agent and tax gatherer were strangers to him, they did not molest or make him afraid, and being thus fortified, he was content to let the producers of wealth eke out a miserable existence while he fared sumptuously every day. But it was not the American capitalist alone who entered into this murderous scheme for demonetizing silver. In the *Banker's Magazine* of August, 1873, we find the following on this subject :

> In 1872, silver being demonetized in France, England and Holland, a capital of $500,000 was raised, and Ernest Seyd of London was sent to this country with this fund, as agent of the foreign bond holders and capitalists, to effect the same object (demonetization of silver), which was accomplished.

There you have it, a paid agent of English capitalists sent to this country with $500,000 to buy the American Congress and rob the American people. In corroboration of this testimony we read from the *Congressional Globe* of April 9,1872, page 2804, these words :

> Ernest Seyd of London, a distinguished writer and bullionist, who is now here, has given great attention to the subject of mint and coinage. After having examined the first draft of this bill (for the demonetization of silver) he made various sensible suggestions, which the committee adopted and embodied in the bill.

So says Mr. Hooper, who, at that time, was chairman of the committee on coinage, but I will further add that I heard Hon. Gilbert De Lamartyr say that Judge Kelly told him that he (Kelly) saw the original draft of the bill for the demonetization of silver, and it was in Ernest Seyd's own handwriting. God of our fathers ! A British capitalist sent here to make laws for the American people. England failed to subjugate us by the bullet, but she stole into our Congressional halls and by the crafty use of gold, obtained possession of the ballot, and today, American industry pays tribute to England, despite our blood-bought seal of independence.

Not only did the demonetization of silver prevent, or at least retard the payment of the bonds, but it added to the value of the gold in which these bonds were then to be paid. Every dollar taken from circulation adds to the value of that which is left, hence the demonetization of silver increases the value of gold. After England had demonetized silver, our silver dollar, containing 412½ grains, was not worth as much in that country by at least ten cents on the dollar, as our gold dollar containing 25.8 grains of gold. By destroying the money value of silver, bonds became payable in gold only, thus adding immensely to their value. A British capitalist, holding $100.000,000 of our four per cent bonds, received an annual interest of $4,000,000, which paid in standard silver would be worth ten per cent, or $400,000 less than it would be if paid in gold. This would make a difference in his daily interest of $1,096. Is it not clear why English capitalists were anxious for the United States to demonetize silver, and why they could afford to send Ernest Seyd to this country with a capital of $500,000 to accomplish this object ?

Just here will the reader stop for a moment and consider why the Rothschilds, who control the financial policy of England, as the brokers and security-holders of America control ours, why they could afford to pay, not only the paltry half -million with which they bought the demonetization of silver, but many millions more had it been necessary ? Our civil war opened the eyes of England. She knew that her welfare nay, almost her existence, depended upon America's supply of cotton, meat and cereals ; these were liable to fail, either in rebellion at home or in war with foreign nations. But she was the world's great creditor, for she held the bonds of all nations, and if she could make them payable in the dearest money in the world, it would enhance her securities many millions, and if she could insure herself an ample supply of wheat and cotton she would be independent of us under all circumstances. Now, since she owned and controlled all India, that great wheat and cotton country, she saw that, with India's cheap labor and the demonetization of American silver, she would have a double leverage over America and her productions. Silver money is used exclusively in India. England coins that money, and if, with eighty cents, she could buy silver, stamp and pass it for a dollar in payment for India's wheat and cotton, she not only gained the 20 per cent from her own subjects, but in consequence of the demonetization of silver in America, her debtors here were compelled to pay her at least ten per cent more than they would have paid had not silver been demonetized. Let it also be borne in mind that this discount, whether much or little, was so much new capital with which to open up the interior of India to compete with America and her productions.

The injury to the people of this country through the demonetization of silver can never, perhaps, be justly estimated. The panic of 1873 which ensued, was one of the most disastrous that ever befell any people. Language fails in a description of the blighting misery that desolated the country ; the ravages of war are scarcely comparable with it. From the demonetization of silver, in 1873, to its remonetization in 1878, may well be called the dark days of our Republic. Bankruptcies and financial disaster brought in train their legitimate offspring ; and the statistics of those and the ensuing years are voluminous with the most startling and loathsome crimes. Murder, insanity, suicide, divorce, drunkenness and all forms of immorality and crime have increased from that day to this in the most appalling ratio. Will any man say that legislation has had nothing to do with the startling increase of crime in our country ? Every result is produced from certain causes, and it is certain that no more like begets like than that the increase of misery and crime in our country are the direct results of evil legislation. And it is impossible for a nation long to remain free whose laws are made granting special privileges to the few and ignoring the rights of the many. The contraction of the currency, commencing with the destruction of the greenbacks in 1866, and the stringency increased by the demonetization of silver in 1873, has been productive of more misery and crime to the people of this country than all the wars, pestilence and famine with which they have ever been afflicted.

In regard to the policy of contraction, Prof. Walker, of Yale College, who is not a politician, nor a statesman, but a cool, unbiased writer and teacher, says :

> When the process of contraction commences, the first class on which it
> falls is the merchants of the large cities, they find it difficult to get money
> to pay their notes ; the next class is the manufacturer, the sale of his goods
> at once falls off ; laborers and mechanics next feel the pressure, they are
> thrown out of employment ; and, lastly, the farmer finds a dull sale for his
> produce ; and all, unsuspicious of the real cause, have a vague idea that
> their difficulties are owing to the hard times. * * We have become so
> familiar with these periodical revolutions in trade, that we look upon them
> as the natural phenomenon of business, but it is not so.

Ricardo, another eminent writer on political economy, says :

> That commodities rise in price in proportion to the increase or diminution
> of money, I hold to be a fact that is incontrovertible.

John Stewart Mill says :

> If the whole volume of money in circulation were doubled, prices would
> double.

The money commission, created August 15, 1876, consisting of three United States Senators, three members of the House, and three secretaries, made a report March 2, 1877, in which appear these words :

> " That the disasters of the Dark Ages were caused by decreasing money and falling prices, and that the recovery therefrom and the comparative prosperity which followed the discovery of America were due to an increasing supply of the precious metal and rising prices, will not seem surprising or unreasonable when the noble functions of money are considered. Money is the great instrument of association, the very fiber of social organism, the vitalizing force of industry, the protoplasm of civilization and as essential to its existence as oxygen is to animal life. Without money civilization could not have had a beginning, and with a diminishing supply it must languish and unless *relieved finally perish.*"
>
> " Falling prices and misery and destitution are inseparable companions." It is universally conceded that falling prices result from the contraction of the money volume. *U.S. Monetary Commission, Vol. 1, p. 50.*

Again p. 51, " The highest moral, intellectual and material development of nations is promoted by the use of money, unchanging in its value."

Here we have the conclusion of nine prominent statesmen, who, after an exhaustive examination, emphatically declare that the "true and only cause" of the calamities that have befallen the people is "the shrinkage in the volume of money." To whom, then, shall we charge these calamities that have come upon us like a flood ? Is it the extravagance of the people ? Is it because too many of the necessaries of life have been produced ? Because the farmer has been too industrious and prudent, or the manufacturer employed too many laborers in the production of his commodities ? Is it because millions of children are employed in the mines and factories of the country, denied every blessing and privilege of childhood ? Is it because the dram shop is sucking away the sustenance of thousands of families, and bringing desolation into their homes ? Is it because women are selling their souls to keep their bodies from starving, or because a band of train robbers are infesting the country and sending terror into the hearts of the people ? No, it is none of these circumstances that have brought such disaster upon our country, but it is a selfish and criminal legislation that has overwhelmed us with these alarming conditions.

When the fiend of civil war was desolating the land, when the great heart of the nation throbbed in agony, and the people were bowed in mourning, then a band of men, with murderous purposes, went, not into the battlefield, but into the very sanctuary of our country, the holy place of government, and there, under the guise of patriot and benefactor, pillaged the soldier, and plotted the most diabolical scheme of robbery that ever blackened a historic page. Who were these men ? Ah, history is writing their names in a most damning record, they are drenched with the blood of martyred children, and the agonizing cry of forty millions of enslaved people is ascending continually day and night. Do you ask for evidence that this people were deliberately robbed by a band of men at the head of our government, who were in league with the money power of Europe ? If so, please read and ponder the "confidential" circular which was issued in 1862 by English capitalists, who commissioned one Hazzard, a London banker, to propagate its principles among American bankers with a view of having the financial legislation of Congress pave the way for its final adoption as the settled policy of this nation. How well they succeeded is best told by millions of wrecked fortunes and ruined homes. Here is the infernal document :

> Slavery is likely to be abolished by the war power, and chattel slavery destroyed. This, I and my European friends are in favor of, for slavery is but the owning of labor, and carries with it the care for the laborer ; while the European plan, led on by England, is capital control of labor, by controlling wages. This can be done by controlling the money. The great debt that capitalists will see to it is made out of the war, must be used as a measure to control the volume of money. To accomplish this the bonds must be used as a banking basis. We are now waiting to get the secretary of the treasury to make his recommendation to Congress. It will not do to allow the greenback, as it is called, to circulate as money any length of time, for we cannot control that.

About the middle of the present century Sir John Lubbock, of England, declared :

> There is likely to be an effort made by the capital class to fasten upon the world a rule through their wealth, *and by means of reduced wages* place the masses upon a footing more degrading and dependent than has ever been known in history. The spirit of money-worshippers seems to be rapidly developing in this direction.

A few years later Abraham Lincoln reiterated the same sentiment in his message to Congress in 1861. (See Barrett's Life of Lincoln, pages 309 and 310.) This important warning is ommitted in the later histories :

> Monarchy itself is sometimes hinted at as a possible refuge from the power of the people. In my present position I could scarcely be justified were I to omit raising a warning voice against the approach of returning despotism. There is one point to which I ask a brief attention. It is the effort to place *capital* on an equal footing with, if not above *labor*, in the structure of government. * * Let them beware of surrendering a political power which they already have, and which, if surrendered, will surely be used to close the door of advancement against such as they, and to fix new disabilities and burdens upon them, till all of liberty shall be lost.

These are the words of warning from our country's sainted martyr, but alas, how little heeded.

Again near the close of the war, in reply to a letter from a friend in Illinois, President Lincoln said :

> Yes we may all congratulate ourselves that this cruel war is nearing its close. It has cost a vast amount of treasure and blood. The best blood of the flower of American youth has been freely offered upon our country's altar that the nation might live. It has been indeed a trying hour for the republic ; but I see in the near future, a crisis approaching that unnerves me and causes me to tremble for the safety of my country.
>
> As a result of the war corporations have been enthroned and an era of corruption in high places will follow, and the money power of the country will endeavor to prolong its reign by working upon the prejudices of the people until all wealth is aggregated in a few hands, and the Republic is destroyed. I feel at this moment more anxiety for the safety of my country than ever before, even in the midst of war. God grant that my suspicions may prove groundless.

What a wonderful prophecy, and how terribly it is being fulfilled.

CHAPTER VIII.
RESUMPTION.

WOULD to God that the record of atrocities against this nation might end here ! But no, with the people crushed and staggering beneath the burdens imposed upon them through the preceding robberies, we next find these vampires in Congress inflicting a seventh scourge upon the people by means of the resumption act.

This act, passed January 14, 1875, authorized the secretary of the treasury to destroy the fractional currency, and issue silver coin in like denominations to take its place. The people had found the fractional currency convenient, not only as a medium of exchange at home, but especially cheap and convenient for small remittances in trade. The destruction of this money was a serious injury to the business men of the country. For without fractional currency, even small remittances incurred the expense of a draft or money order. But Congress appeared to be looking after the interest of the money-monger and not to the prosperity of the country.

It next became necessary to issue bonds with which to purchase the silver bullion authorized for coinage. Let it be remembered that these were untaxed, interest-bearing bonds, and of such large denominations that only capitalists were able to carry them, while to the debt-ridden people was added the interest of these very bonds, which could only exist by the destruction of the greenbacks and fractional currency upon which the people paid no interest.

The restoration of silver as a medium of exchange was a great triumph to the unthinking masses and greatly increased their confidence in the governmental policy, but to those who studied the situation the jingle of silver was another death-knell to the prosperity of the country. Is it not clear that by destroying a non-interest bearing currency, as the greenback, and substituting an interest bearing bond, that a burden has been added to the people ? Not to the tax-payer only, but to every consumer of food and clothing. But farther, not only has the resumption of specie added to the burdens of the people, but the whole system is a miserable farce. The people have been told, and the masses believe, that their paper currency is redeemable in specie. But first, the smallest amount redeemable is fifty dollars, and secondly, the only place of redemption is the sub-treasury in the city of New York. Is not this clearly another scheme to advance the interests of Shylock ? The expense of getting to the sub-treasury, together with the large amount required, at once shuts off the masses from any advantage there might be in resumption. The people are told that the national bank currency is redeemable in greenbacks, and the greenbacks in specie ; but the fact is carefully concealed that there is not specie enough behind the paper currency to redeem one-half of it ; and should a crisis arise which gave any advantage to the holders of coin, Shylock would be first at the sub-treasury, while the masses with less than fifty dollars at their command would be compelled to lose any advantage there might be in resumption. Will some "hard money" philosopher rise and explain wherein *the people* have been benefited by resumption ? But it does not require a philosopher to show wherein their burdens have been increased through this infamous scheme.

John Sherman who was once honest and then opposed this measure, predicted the results in a speech made in 1869, as follows :

> It is not possible to take this voyage without the sorest distress. To every person except a capitalist out of debt, or a salaried officer, or annuitant, it is a period of loss, danger, lassitude of trade, fall of wages, suspension of enterprise, bankruptcy, and disaster. * * It means the ruin of all dealers whose debts are twice their business capital, though one-third less than their actual property. It means the fall of all agricultural productions without any great reduction of taxes. When that day comes, every man, as the sailor says, will be close reefed, all enterprise will be suspended, every bank will have contracted its currency to the lowest limit ; and the debtor, compelled to meet in coin a debt contracted in currency, will find the coin hoarded in the treasury, no representative of coin in circulation, his property shrunk not only to the extent of the appreciation of the currency, but still more by the artificial scarcity made by the holders of gold. To attempt this task by a surprise upon our people by arresting them in the midst of their lawful business and applying a new standard of value to their property, without any reduction of their debts, or giving them an opportunity to compound with their creditors, or to distribute the losses, would be an act of folly without an example in evil in modern times.

These were the evils that would follow resumption, as prophesied by John Sherman before the clutch of the money power had dwarfed and blackened his soul. Quick to perceive the right with an intuitive love of justice, John Sherman was the natural friend of the people, but avarice perverting his nature, we find him the ready tool of the money power, bartering away his instinctive love of justice and relentlessly antagonizing the interests of the people. His prophecies remain, however, and their fulfillment is undying witness against his degenerate soul.

Beasey says :

> Slavery is the inevitable result of poverty ; poverty is the inevitable result of low wages ; low wages are the inevitable result of scarcity of currency and an improper system of taxation ; and scarcity of currency and an improper system of taxation are the logical results of an unjust administration of the government.

Besides the testimony of Senator Sherman and Beasey against the infamous measure, I will also add the opinion of Senator Ferry, of Michigan, who, too honest to retract and take issue against the great industrial masses, paid the penalty perscribed by President Grant, and is no longer " entrusted in public place." Here are the words of Senator Ferry in regard to resumption and contraction :

It is easy to see why moneyed men want contraction ; the shrinkage then which others must suffer would find compensation in their expanded purses. It would be robbing Peter (the people) to pay Paul (the millionaire).

Never were truer words uttered ; the shrinkage which followed contraction ruined thousands, while the moneyed class, without an effort, actually doubled their wealth. Again Senator Ferry says :

> The universal distres and unparalled failures which have followed these past years of trial, must sadly record the severity of the process, which has brought the country so near resumption and so close to financial ruin.

Through the process of contraction, all the truths stated by Senator Ferry have been verified, and all the evils predicted by Senator Sherman have befallen this people. Nor is this the end, for the train of evils brought upon us through this infernal legislation is sapping the energies of the nation and rapidly undermining the bulwarks of our Republic. But it is not necessary to quote the opinions of statesmen, politicians, or political economists to prove that the contraction of our currency has been disastrous to our national prosperity. The experience of the American people for the last twenty years has demonstrated most terribly and conclusively that any system of contraction of the currency is fatal to the industry, morality and general prosperity of a nation.

According to treasury reports for the last fiscal year there is, all told, in the United States $1,394,781,000 cash. On January, 1876, Treasurer Jordan reported in the United States treasury $601,102,318.10 (page 45), since that date the hoard has increased at least $100,000,000. He also reported in banks $369,475,385. Total locked up, $1,070,577,703, leaving among the people in circulation $324,103,297. This, divided among 60,000,000 of people, gives us the per capita of each the sum of $5.40. At the close of the war we had in circulation about $2,000,000,000, including the three per cent treasury certificates, compound interest notes, and 7-30 bonds, which entered into the circulating medium ; and a population of about 40,000,000, this sum divided up gave a per capita to each of about $50. Nearly ten times as much per capita as we have at present. With these figures before us who can doubt the real cause of business stagnation, and the rapid increase of pauperism and crime ?

Every farmer knows how much more wheat, hay, pork, corn, or wool it takes to *buy a dollar* now than it did at the close of the war, and many of them know by bitter experience how a mortgage of a few hundred or thousand dollars has swallowed up twice that amount invested in houses, lands or any other property except bonded securities. While property in the form of bonds, mortgages, and stocks, has rapidly appreciated in value, every other form of property has depreciated in the same ratio. Only the wealthy classes are able to hold bond, mortgage and stock securities, and for twenty-five years the great struggles in Congress have been to appreciate the value of these investments, which could only be done by depreciating the property of the masses. Consequently we have found the rich amassing colossal fortunes while the laboring classes are sinking to lower and lower depths of degradation. Since a man's social, intellectual and moral status depends largely upon his material prosperity, is not that legislation to be denounced which impoverishes the masses, thus degrading them in all the relations of life ?

CHAPTER IX.
CONCLUSION.

WE have now completed a brief outline of seven atrocious conspiracies against this government ; conspiracies which for boldness of purpose and cruelty of design, are without a parallel in the annals of crime, and all perpetrated within the brief period of thirteen years ; thirteen years in which the powers of darkness sat enthroned in our national capitol ; thirteen years of utter disregard for the rights of the people ; thirteen years in which class-legislation gave birth to more moneyed and monopolistic powers than ever before cursed any civilized people.

Will it be said I have made misstatements in these charges ? In repiy I only ask that you search the official records in corroboration of what is contained in these pages. I challenge contradiction of the truths set forth in this little volume. Political tricksters may distort these truths ; capitalists may sneer and public opinion derisively shake its head, but the *truths* remain, and their results are stamped in burning characters upon the heart of a dying nation. The record of the American Congress from February 25, 1862, to January 24, 1875, is a record of the blackest and most heartless crimes. But kind reader, do not for one moment deceive yourself with the thought that this corrupt legislation ceased on that memorable day. Ah, no ; the act of resumption simply completed the infernal machinery by which the money power is crushing out the liberty and lives of the American people. By controlling the finances of the country they have been enabled to form trusts and syndicates which have reduced the people to a wage-slavery more abject and heartless than any chattel slavery that ever cursed God's earth.

The people having slept until this machinery was perfected, have at last awakened from their dream of freedom to find their liberties fettered, and themselves in the grasp of a system of monopolies whose Titanic enginery is crushing out not only liberty, but life itself. And when we consider the fact that the representatives of these monopolies sit in our congressional halls and practically control the United States Senate, that highest law-making power in the land, who does not tremble for the safety not only of our Republic, but of our civilization. The results of this legislation are being universally realized, and fears may justly be entertained that we have already passed the point beyond which our steps may be retraced and our liberties retrieved.

Yes, the people are awakening, but the money power is on guard, they have entrenched themselves at every available point, and are now clamoring for an appropriation to establish a military power. Let us not be deceived ; this cry for an established militia is not to defend ourselves against a foreign foe ; the enemy is within our gates, sitting in the high places of our country. They tell us "the wealth of the country must be protected." Ah, the *wealth of the country requires protection*. It is not labor they would protect ; it is not the oppressed they would have go free, it is not the burden of toil they would lighten, but the *wealth* of the country demands protection. But what is this wealth that cannot be protected without military force ? Ah, sirs, it is that wealth of which the people have been robbed ; it is the ill-gotten gain of a moneyed oligarchy. It is not the fear of foreign invaders, not the fear that the masses will violate law, but that they will repeal unjust statutes, and restore to the people the inheritance of which they have been so outrageously robbed. Where these robberies will end it is hardly possible to conjecture, but the light is breaking, for God in the multitude of his mercies has raised up a band of sturdy men to stay the dark waters that are overwhelming this people. For twelve years this little Spartan band has stood guard at the mystic pass that leads down to national death. For twelve years the old party Goliaths have stood in awe of this band of Davids, and God has strengthened their arms and multiplied their numbers until there is no place in all this land where their voice is not heard, and where their words do not cause hope to spring up in the hearts of the oppressed.

But spurred on by his appetite for plunder, Shylock still dares to raise his murderous hand against this people. Greed is never satisfied, its ill-gotten gains only serve to sharpen its appetite, and it is ever crying *more*, MORE. Cunning hands, schemeing brains, degenerate souls, still plot the destruction of this Republic. Their next plan is to destroy the $346,000,000 of greenbacks, which have only been preserved thus far through the untiring vigilance in our national Congress of such men as Weaver, Gillette and the devoted DeLamartyr, aided by the purse, pen and brains of such men as Peter Cooper, Clover, Swinton, West, Norton, Harper, Heath, Berkey, Phillips, Martin, Polk, and an innumerable host whose names are enshrined in the hearts of a grateful people.

Besides the destruction of the greenbacks it is their settled policy to rob us of the silver dollar and place our currency upon a single gold basis. This is another diabolic scheme solely in the interest of the creditor class.

There is not, there cannot be a greater enemy to American producers than John Sherman and that class of men who are devoting all their energies to the destruction of silver as money. With gold as a basis and the banks to issue the paper currency of the country, the people would be entirely at the mercy of Shylock. Indeed, are we not already at the feet of the money power ?

The New York *Tribune*, under the management of Whitelaw Reid, said :

> The time is near when they (the banks) will feel compelled to act
> strongly. Meanwhile a very good thing has been done. The machinery is
> now furnished by which, in any emergency, the financial corporations of
> the east can act together on a single day's notice with such power that no
> act of Congress can overcome or resist their decision.

Shades of Horace Greeley ! Can it be possible that the New York *Tribune*, that once powerful advocate of justice, has become so perverted as to call it "a very good thing," that the financial corporations of the east are furnished with the machinery whereby they can control Congress. Where are we, then ? Is it the financial corporations of the east, or the United States Congress, that govern this country ? The New York *Tribune*, that grand old anti-slavery champion, says it is "the financial corporations of the east," and rejoices in it as "a very good thing."

What, then, avail the words of Horace Greeley, or the blood of a million martyred soldiers, or the expenditure of five billions of treasure ? Have we not today fifty millions of people under the bondage of financial corporations ? A bondage more galling and more heartless than that beneath the lash of southern slavery—more galling because perpetrated in the name of liberty, more heartless because there is none to heed the cries of the starving white slaves, none to pity them dying, none to bury their dead. The shackles were dropped from four millions of black slaves, not to make them free, but to enslave the whole producing industries of the country, through this infernal bond and bank scheme.

History proves that nothing has been so disastrous to nations as the enactment of laws which favor the few at the expense of the many. There is no robbery so suicidal as that sanctioned by law ; for it not only destroys the morality of the legalized robber, starves and kills the victimized masses, but it degrades the law-maker himself to a level with the most notorious highwayman. Ruskin says : " The occult theft, theft that hides itself even from itself, and is legal, respectable and cowardly, corrupts the body and soul of man to the very last fibre of them." And history proves that such legislation destroys nations, degrades humanity, and is a mockery against the most high God. Against the Eternal Judge who will not hold guiltless him who lends a voice to such iniquitous legislation. A legislation that destroys both soul and body of the toiling millions.

CHAPTER X.
SHERMAN VERSUS EMERY.

John Davis Replies to the Hon. Sherman's Latest Letter on Finance.

Since the days of John Brown, Kansas has never ceased to be the stamping ground of reform. Ushered into statehood on the eve of a terrible civil war, her baptism in blood fitted her peculiarly for the growth of liberty and equality.

Never since the days of John Brown have the liberty loving men of Kansas ceased in their determination to hallow the soil made sacred by the life and death of their illustrious martyr.

That soil harrowed by the intelligence of truth loving men and fertilized by the blood of thousands of patriotic soldiers, was well fitted to receive the seeds of historic truth embodied in Seven Financial Conspiracies, and when in the campaign of 1888 fifty thousand copies of the little book were scattered broadcast over the state, the enemies of freedom seeing that it would yield an everlasting harvest to liberty, rushed forth and attempted to destroy the sower and the seed.

Preparatory to their onslaught their chiefs met in council and evolved two monumental documents which were launched upon the public under the captaincy of Messrs. Ady and Kelley.

Again in the campaign of 1891 when ten thousand of these little messengers were scattered over Ohio, the book and its author were again assailed.

The veritable John Sherman whose villainous acts had made possible such a record of crime induced by the solicitude of his political friends came out with an open letter published in the Cincinnati Enquirer and addressed to Chas. F. Stokey of Canton, O., in which he denounces the book as "wild and visionary," and declares that the Shylock to which the author alludes is a "phantom of her imagination."

The documents of Ady and Kelley, as also the letter of Senator Sherman were immediately met by the indomitable John Davis through the columns of his paper *The Junction City* (Kan.) *Tribune*.

These replies of Mr. Davis are so replete with historic truth that we present the one in reply to Senator Sherman for the consideration of our readers :

A few years ago Mrs. S.E.V. Emery of Michigan emptied a quiver of arrows into the ranks of the people's enemies. The darts seemed light and feathery, and the bow string was drawn by the weak arm of a woman. Yet the shafts were winged and pointed with truth and justice, and the woman's arm was nerved with an earnest patriotism. Very soon the wounded birds began to flutter and the broken wings were trailing in the dust.

In the year 1888, 50,000 copies of Mrs. Emery's little book were showered among the people of Kansas. Under their fructifying influence the seeds of thought began to spring up in every heart. The rage of the enemy knew no bounds. Great lawyers and judges of courts wrote pamphlets and newspaper broadsides which were circulated by Republican committees and corporation newspapers as campaign documents. Smaller men called the little book "The Union Labor Bible." They cursed it in their speeches, tore it to pieces in he presence of their audiences, dashed it to the floor, spat upon it, trampled it under foot. All this but proved the rage of the lion that had been wounded, the pain of the whale that was pierced, or the bird that was "hit." Next comes the emptying of another quiver of shafts by the same arm that showered Kansas. This time further East. And, promptly, is produced the same results. A Senator of the United States from Ohio deems it worth his while to confess the pain of the arrow in his breast by a review of the situation in the usual corporation attorney style. A copy of that review is before me, over the name of John Sherman. I beg to quote and discuss portions of it :

MANSFIELD, OHIO, Oct. 12, 1891.

Mr. Charles F. Stokey, Canton, Ohio :
MY DEAR SIR—Yours of the 8th, accompanied by Mrs. S.E.V. Emery's pamphlet, called "Seven Financial Conspiracies Which Have Enslaved the American People," is received. Some time since this wild and visionary book was sent to me, and I read it with both amusement and astonishment that any one could read it with approval or be deceived by its falsehoods. The "Seven Financial Conspiracies" are the seven great pillars of our financial credit, the seven great financial measures by which the government was saved from the perils of war and by which the United States has become the most flourishing and prosperous nation in the world. The first chapter attributes the Civil War to an infamous plot of capitalists to absorb the wealth of the country at the expense of the people, when all the world knows that the Civil War was organized by slaveholders to destroy the national government and to setup a slave-holding confederacy in the South upon its ruins. The Shylock described by Mrs. Emery is a phantom of her imagination. The "Shylocks ot the war" were the men who furnished the means to carry on the government and to put down the rebellions and included in their number the most patriotic citizens of the Northern States, who, uniting their means with the services and sacrifices of our soldiers, put down the rebellion, abolished slavery and preserved and strengthened our government. The first of her "conspiracies" she calls the exception clause in the act of February 25, 1862, by which the duties on imported goods were required to be paid in

coin in order to provide the means to pay the interest on our bonds in coin. This clause had not only the cordial support of Secretary Chase, but of President Lincoln, and proved to be the most important financial aid of the government devised during the war. * * * This exception clause saved our public credit by making a market for our bonds and was paid by foreigners for the privilege of entering our markets.

Like most men with a bad case on hand, the Senator appears to have little regard for truth, and sets out with a misstatement. Mrs. Emery's book does not "attribute the Civil War to all infamous plot of capitalists," etc. The book plainly states (page 11) that "African slavery" was the cause of secession and consequent war. Mrs. Emery and the Senator agree as to the cause of the Civil War, and both state it plainly in their own words, about which there can be no disagreement. Mrs. Emery then takes the ground that the great capitalists were pleased with the opportunity to speculate on the needs of the country, and that they proceeded to profit by the situation, as we shall see in the course of this discussion. The little book uses plain language to suit the plain common people, and hence calls the London and Wall Street speculators "Shylocks." This the Senator condemns, saying that "the Shylocks of the war were the men who furnished the means to carry on the government," etc., as above quoted. In this matter Mrs. Emery is in good company.

She agrees with Thaddeus Stevens, Senator Wilson, Andrew Jackson, Thomas Jefferson, Senator Benton and others in calling men and things by their proper names. But this will appear more plainly in the course of the discussion. I now call attention to the Senator's remarks concerning the First Financial Conspiracy.

Fortunately we are not left in the dark as to the causes and agencies which placed the exception clause on the greenback. Prominent actors in the matter have left their words and acts on record.

The legal tender Bill was introduced in the House by E.G. Spaulding of Buffalo, N.Y., Chairman of the Sub-committee of Ways and Means, December 31, 1861. It was discussed in the House, and perfected, until February 6, 1862. It passed the House by a vote of 93 to 59. It provided for a full legal-tender money with no exception clauses.

After passing the House, the Legal-tender Bill went to the Senate. The Senate amended the bill by providing that the contemplated money should be legal tender for all purposes "except duties on imports and interest on the public debt." Mrs. Emery claims that those exceptions were the work of the bankers. Mr. Stevens, Chairman of the Ways and Means Committee—the grand old "commoner" from Pennsylvania—tells how the crime of wounding the greenback was committed :

TESTIMONY OF THADDEUS STEVENS.

MR. SPEAKER :—I have a very few words to say. I approach the subject with more depression of spirits than I ever approached any question. No personal motive influences me. I hope not at least. I have a melancholy foreboding that we are about to consummate a cunningly-devised scheme, which will carry great injury and great loss to all classes of people throughout this Union, except one. With my colleague, I believe that no act of legislation was ever hailed with as much delight throughout the length and breadth of this Union, by every class of people without exception, as the bill which we passed and sent to the Senate. Congratulations from all classes—merchants, traders, manufacturers, mechanics and laborers—poured in upon us from all quarters. The Boards of Trade from Boston, New York, Philadelphia, Cincinnati, Louisville, St. Louis, Chicago and Milwaukee approved its provisions and urged its passage as it was. I have a dispatch from the Chamber of Commerce, Cincinnati, sent to the Treasurer, and by him to me, urging the speedy passage of the bill as it passed the House. It is true there was a doleful sound came up from the caverns of bullion brokers and from the salons of the associated banks. Their cashiers and agents were soon on the ground and persuaded the Senate, with but little deliberation, to mangle and destroy what it had cost the House months to digest, consider and pass. They fell upon the bill in hot haste, and so disfigured and deformed it that its father would not know it. Instead of being a beneficient and invigorating measure, it is positively mischievous. It has all the bad qualities which its enemies charged on the original bill, and none of its benefits. It now creates money, and by its very terms declares it a depreciated currency. It makes two classes of money : one for banks and brokers, and another for the people. It discriminates between the rights of different classes of creditors, allowing the capitalists to demand gold, and compelling the ordinary lender of money on individual security to receive notes which the government had purposely discredited. * * * * * * All classes of people shall take these legal-tender notes at par for every article of trade or contract, unless they have money enough to buy United States bonds, and then they shall be paid in gold. Who is that favored class ? The banks and brokers and nobody else.

—*Speech in House, February 20, 1862.*

That is the statement of the chairman of the committee that originated the bill. He and Mrs. Emery agree that the brokers and bankers are responsible for the exception clause that depreciated the greenback money.

Senator Sherman says it is one of the great pillars of our financial credit.

TESTIMONY OF HENRY WILSON.

It is a contest between the brokers, jobbers and moneychangers on the one side, and the people of the United States on the other. I venture to express the opinion that ninety-nine of every hundred of the loyal people of the United States are for this legal-tender clause.

—*Wilson's Speech in the Senate, February 13, 1862.*

THE VOICE OF HISTORY.

The [legal tender] bill was no sooner made public than delegations of bankers from New York, Boston and Philadelphia hurried to Washington to oppose it. They organized in a formal manner by selecting a chairman (S.A. Mercer of Philadelphia), and invited the finance Committee of the Senate and the Committee of Ways and Means of the House to meet them at the office of the Secretary of the Treasury January 11, 1862. The invitation was accepted. At the meeting which followed the bankers spoke in opposition to the bill. * * * The bank delegates remained in Washington and held further consultation with Secretary Chase extending through several days, which resulted in an arrangement with him to the effect, among other things, that Congress should be urged to pass the National Bank Bill, etc.

—*Berkey's Monetary System, 1876.*

TESTIMONY OF WM. D. KELLEY.

I remember the grand old commoner Thaddeus Stevens, with his hat in his hand and his cane under his arm, when he returned to the House after his final conference (on the exception clause) and shedding bitter tears over the result. "Yes," said he, "we had to yield ; the Senate was stubborn. We did not yield until we found that the country must be lost or the banks gratified, and we have sought to save the country in spite of the cupidity of its wealthier citizens."

Judge Wm. D. Kelley, Philadelphia, January 15, 1876.

Let us now analyze the vote on the Legal-tender Bill. When voted on in the House on its first passage, authorizing a full legal-tender money, it passed by a vote of 93 to 59. Among the voters in the majority we find the names of Stevens, Spaulding, Windom, Wilson, Hale, Fessenden, Colfax, Bingham, Hooper and a majority of the great Union Congressmen, who were then in favor of a full legal-tender currency. In the minority, we find Vallandigham, Voorhees, Pendleton, Wm.H. English and S.S. Cox. Vallandigham of Ohio was very emphatic in his denunciation of legal-tender paper. He said :

> Cheap in materials, easy of issue, worked by steam, signed by machinery, there will be no end to the legion of paper devils which shall pour forth from the loins of the Secretary.

Vallandigham insisted that these notes were not money, that they would not circulate as money :

> Though you should send them forth bearing ten times the image and superscription—the fair face and form of ABRAHAM LINCOLN, now President and CÆSAR of the American Republic. * * * I utterly deny, sir, the right of the Federal government to provide a paper currency, intended primarily to circulate as money and meet the demands of business and commercial transactions and to the exclusion of all other paper.

But when the bill was returned from the Senate, mutilated and depreciated by the infamous exception clause, we find Vallandigham, Voorhees, Cox, Pendleton, English, *et hoc genus omne*, voting for the mutilated bill authorizing a crippled and depreciated money. * * * They did not agree with Secretary Chase, Wilson, Stevens, Hale and Windom, those great and noble patriots who tried to give to the country a legal-tender money without any mutilation and exceptions ; and as these men who have been styled "traitors" voted in the House, so voted John Sherman in the Senate. Neither Sherman, Vallandigham nor Voorhees agreed with Secretary Chase, Wilson, Stevens, Hale, Windom and all those great and noble patriots who tried to give to the country a legal-tender money without any mutilations and exceptions. (*See Spaulding's History, 1869*).

The object of the exception clause on the greenback was to cause its depreciation so that the holders of gold could buy up the currency at half-price and then invest it in bonds at face value. Senator Sherman himself once explained the whole matter in a single sentence. He said : " It became necessary to depreciate the notes in order to create a market for the bonds." That is, the great rich men, whom Thomas Jefferson called " the traitorous class," would not invest in the bonds unless they could double their money by so doing.

Having beaten the government in the exception-clause fight, which Mr. Stevens called "the first victory of the money power over the country," the Shylocks determined to take further advantage of the necessities of the government and the exigencies of the times. So in 1863 they procured the passage of

THE NATIONAL BANKING LAW.

Under this law the bondholders could place the bonds which had cost them about 50 cents on the dollar, in the United States Treasury, without sacrificing any of the interest-income, and receive back 90 per cent of the bonds in bank currency to loan to the people, as bankers. This gave the bankers two interest-incomes from one investment. With $50,000 in gold they could become the happy owners of $100,000 of interest-bearing bonds and $90,000 of currency, all free from taxes "under State or local authority." This was a big bonanza, or, in fact, two bonanzas combined. This law was passed during one of the darkest periods of the war, when patriots, statesmen, generals, soldiers and people were straining every nerve to save the country. It pounced upon its prey like a panther when the victim was bleeding at every pore. Moulton's *History of American Finances,* page 131, states the case as follows :

> Mr. Sherman now introduced the National Bank Bill. After a lengthy debate, it passed the Senate by a vote of 23 to 21. In the meantime there had been several bills for the same purpose introduced and referred to the committee in the House. When the Senate Bill came down it was not referred, as usual, but brought before the House without consideration in committee with other similar bills. It was not discussed in Committee of the Whole, but under a motion to refer, which cut off all amendments, the friends of the bill debated its general merits. When by parliamentary tactics it was forced to a final vote, it passed under the gag rule of the previous question by a vote of 78 to 64.

And thus was fulfilled the prediction of Senator Thos. Benton, when, on the victory of President Jackson over the United States Bank, said that Jackson had beaten the bank ; yet the bank power was not conquered, but, like a "royal tiger" driven to the jungles, he will return again. He returned in 1863 to prey upon the prostrate form of a bleeding Republic, when neither President, Congress nor people had the power to resist his coming. With 3,000 whelps and an aggregate capital of $700,000,000, much of it furnished by the government, this "ROYAL TIGER" has been for twenty-five years preying upon the fortunes and liberties of the people, through this system of legalized robbery.

Seven times the people of the United States have voted on this national bank question at Presidential elections. Five times out of the seven they declared, by their votes, that "a national bank is unconstitutional and dangerous to liberty." That sentiment was a regular plank in Democratic platforms prior to 1860, and five times that platform was approved by the people at the Presidential elections.

Peter Cooper tells us that, in 1793, President Washington signed a resolution of the American Senate declaring that a holder of bank stock should not have a seat in Congress. And when John Quincy Adams was elected to Congress he refused to qualify until he had disposed of his bank stock. And yet Senator Sherman is in favor of the national banking system, and his party regularly send to the United States Senate numerous bank presidents, just as if this great country has no other interests worth attention except stock gambling, coupon clipping and usury collecting.

And at this moment the President of the United States Senate is not only a banker, but a BRITISH BANKER, doing business in London as "Morton, Rose & Co." And, further, should President Harrison die, we would have a LONDON BANKER AS PRESIDENT OF THE UNITED STATES ! Verily Thomas Jefferson was right when he said : "Banking institutions are more dangerous than standing armies."

The exception clause on the Greenback Bill and the national banking law are all the "conspiracies" mentioned in Mrs. Emery's book that were enacted during the administration of President Lincoln. I have shown that they were perpetrated by the money power while Mr. Lincoln and the country were so terribly pressed by the exigencies of the war that Mr. Lincoln had no option or responsibility in the matter. He submitted to them under coercion ; he approved them to placate one enemy while he battled with another ; being unable, as he himself said, on one occassion, to fight two wars at once. He submitted to the inevitable, as Washington, Jefferson, Adams, Henry and other champions of liberty in their day submitted to the existence of slavery and the slave trade—because there was no other alternative !

It will be remembered that Secretary Chase favored the legal-tender law, and that it required several days of meetings and threats of financial coercion by the "bank delegates," who "remained in Washington" after the exception clause, to induce Mr. Chase to recommend the bank law. Mr. Chase lived long enough to bitterly regret the part he took in the matter, and is reported as expressing himself as follows :

> My agency in procuring the passage of the National Bank Act was the greatest financial mistake of my life. It has built up a monopoly that affects every interest in the country. It should be repealed. But before this can be accomplished, the people will be arrayed on one side and the banks on the other in a contest such as we have never seen in this country.— *Salmon P. Chase.*

To show the undoubted facts in the case, and the usual treason of the money power in all great emergencies, I call the especial attention of Senator Sherman and all Republicans to the following from Senator Ingalls :

> No people in a great emergency ever found a faithful ally in gold. It is the most cowardly and treacherous of all metals. It makes no treaty it does not break. It has no friend it does not sooner or later betray. Armies and Navies are not maintained by gold. In times of panic and calamity, shipwreck and disaster, it becomes the agent and minister of ruin. No nation ever fought a great war by the aid of gold. On the contrary, in the crisis of the greatest peril, it becomes an enemy more potent than the foe

in the field ; but when the battle is won and peace has been secured gold reappears and claims the fruits of victory. In our own Civil War it is doubtful if the gold of New York and London did not work us greater injury than the powder and lead and iron of the South. It was the most invincible enemy of the public credit. Gold paid no soldier or sailor. It refused the national obligations. It was worth most when our fortunes were the lowest. Every defeat gave it increased value. It was in open alliance with our enemies the world over, and all its energies were evoked for our destruction. But as usual, when danger had been averted and the victory secured, gold swaggers to the front and asserts the supremacy.— *Ingall's speech in the United States Senate, February 15, 1878.*

That is a short but fair description of the men whom Mrs. Emery calls "Shylocks." Senator Sherman says they were the men who furnished the means to put down the rebellion. Thomas Jefferson called them the "traitorous class." Senator Wilson called them "brokers, jobbers and money-changers." Thaddeus Stevens called them "bullion brokers;" who sent their cashiers and agents into Congress to influence legislation in their own interest ; also, "sharks and brokers."

It appears, then, that "Shylock" is not "a phantom of Mrs. Emery's brain," but a living reality, who, according to Mr. Spaulding, would only loan his *currency* to the government for big interest, on good security, and interest and principal payable in gold.

Mr. John A. Anderson, an orthodox Republican member of Congress for twelve years, and now Consul General to Cairo under the present Republican administration, said :

By the Charter Act the system was to terminate in twenty years. It was never intended to continue it ; the original design was to stop it at the end of twenty years ; but the power of the banks had then (46th Congress) become greater than that of Congress. The system was not stopped at the end of twenty years, and may now go on forever so far as the original and organic safeguard has anything to do with it.

Senator Sherman's defense of the national banking system is extremely weak. He merely compares it with other banks of issue, and says : " It is now conceded to have been the best form of paper money ever issued by banks that has ever been devised."

Mr. Anderson shows that there need not be any "form of paper money issued by banks," but that the true paper money is the legal-tender greenback, issued by the general government. Mr. Anderson agrees with Thomas Jefferson that "bank currency should be suppressed and the circulation restored to the nation where it belongs."

Senator Sherman dares not controvert that position. He prefers, rather, to erect a man of straw at which to aim his darts. As the old State bank system of paper issues have now no friends he feels very safe in fighting them, in order to justify this "great pillar of our financial credit," which Mr. Anderson says is now too strong for Congress, and which is always on the wrong side in matters of legislation.

The Third "Conspiracy" under discussion is the contraction of the currency. Strange to say, the Senator denied that there has been any contraction, and says :

> It has been demonstrated by official documents that, from the beginning of the war to this time, the volume of our currency has been increasing year by year more rapidly than our population.

This statement is palpably false, as shown by "the official documents" of 1865, 1866 and later, and by the leading Republican speakers, including the Senator himself, Senator Logan and others. Senator Sherman's change of front, between the years 1869 and 1874, was so notorious and shameless that Senator Logan publicly charged him with the change without eliciting a denial.

The Senator tries to sustain his statement of the non-contraction of the currency by the recent falsehood of his party leaders that the 7-30 Treasury notes did not circulate as money.

But Secretary McCullough in his report for December, 1865, says we have now about $2,000,000,000 nearly all in circulation among the people. While in March, 1874, General Logan says "Contraction has gone on until the whole amount of currency of every kind now outstanding is only $742,000,000."

It will be noticed that Secretary McCullough and General Logan both classed the $830,000,000 of 7-30 notes among the active currency of the country, Senator Sherman to the contrary, notwithstanding. In reply to a note of inquiry General Spinner, ex-United States Treasurer, stated as follows :

> MOHAWK, August 17, 1876.
>
> Sir :—Your letter of the 15th inst. has been received. In answer I have to say that the 7-30 notes were intended, prepared, issued and *used* as money.
>
> Very respectfully yours,
> F.E. SPINNER.

Senator Sherman does not agree with McCullough, Logan and Spinner. Who is right ?

I call attention to the following table and remarks from the Chicago *Inter-Ocean*, a leading Republican paper of Illinois in 1878 :

Year.	Currency.	Population.	Per capita
1865	$1,651,282,373	34,819,581	$47.42
1866	1.803.702.726	35.537.148	50.76

1867................ 1,330,414,677	36,269,502	36.68
1868................ 817,199,773	37,016,949	22.08
1869................ 750,025,989	37,779,800	19.85
1870................ 740,039,179	38,588,371	19.19
1871................ 734,244,774	39,750,073	18.47
1872................ 736,340,912	40,978,607	17.97
1873................ 733,291,749	42,245,110	17.48
1874................ 779,031,589	43,550,756	17.89
1875................ 778,176,250	44,896,705	17.33
1876................ 735,358,832	46,284,344	15.89
1877................ . 696,443,394	47,714,829	14.60

The 7-30 three-year notes, whose circulation as currency is most scouted, were outstanding on the, 1st of September, 1865, to the amount of $830,000,000, every dollar of which was legal tender for its face value under the terms of the law, "to the same extent as United States notes."

Secretary Fessenden's report of December 6, 1864, says he caused to be paid out to the soldiers in the field over $20,000,000 of these 7-30 notes at one time.

President U.S. Grant's message of December 2, 1873, indorses the fact of contraction up to the time as follows :

During the last four years the currency has been contracted directly by the withdrawal of the 3 per cent certificates, compound interest notes, and 7-30 bonds outstanding on the 4th of March, 1869 (all of which took the place of legal tenders in bank reserves), to the extent of $63,000,000.

Here is a letter from the president of a national bank and a member of the Forty-third Congress :

OFFICE OF FIRST NATIONAL BANK.

NEW JERSEY, August 12, 1878.

In compliance with your request of the 18 inst., that I should define the relative position of the 7-30 Treasury notes to the general volume of currency in 1865, I have to say that I was then daily in the habit of receiving and paying out the same in the conduct of my ordinary business the same as greenbacks, and I esteemed their peculiar characteristics (being conducive of elasticity) as not only forming a currency, but a currency of special merit.

AMOS CLARK.

Testimony like this may be produced from the official documents of the government and other reliable sources to any desirable extent, and yet, in the face of it all, Senator Sherman says the 7-30 Treasury notes did not circulate as money and that there has been no contraction of the currency !

Senator John A. Logan, in his great speech of March 17, 1874, discussing the panic of 1873, said :

> But, sir, that the panic was not due to the character of the currency is proved by the history of the panic itself. * * * No, sir, the panic was not attributable to the character of the currency, but to a money famine, and to nothing else. In the very midst of the panic we saw the leading bankers and business men of New York pressing and urging the President and the Secretary of the Treasury to let loose twenty or twenty-five millions more of the same paper for their relief. The very same men who today denounce it as a disgrace to our government. It was good enough for them when they were in trouble.

On the subject of the panic of 1873 to 1877, the United States Monetary Commission says :

> The true and only cause of the stagnation in industry and commerce, now everywhere felt, is the fact everywhere existing of falling prices, caused by a shrinking volume of money. * * * * This is the great cause. All others are collateral, cumulative or really the effects of that primal cause. Practical men see what the mischief is, and they all see it alike, and without formulating their ideas into set words and phrases, they state it alike. Capitalists, large and small, give one and only one reason for refusing to invest in productive enterprises. Uniformly and universally the reason given is that prices are falling and may continue to fall, and that money is the best thing to get and hold while that state of things continues. * * * Falling prices, is only another expression for an increasing value of money, by contracting its volume.

In order to throw some light on the question as to who or what class of society is interested in a scanty volume of money and low prices of labor and the products of labor, I call attention to an extract from the *Inter-Ocean* of February 28, 1874, quoted and approved by General Logan in his speech of March 17, 1874. The *Inter-Ocean* said :

> In the national Senate Chamber a bitter contest is in progress by the representatives of the moneyed aristocracy on the one hand, and by the representatives of the masses of the people on the other. The proposition on the part of the capitalists is to grasp and firmly hold the largest possible percentage of the profits of all the labor of the country. They want high rates of interest whereby they may tax traffic, and low rates of wages whereby they may tax labor. By contracting the currency they secure both

of these objects, for they force traffic to supplicate the banks for loans, and drive labor to beggary ; and as the necessities of merchants render more pressing their importunities for loans, the rate of interest is advanced to cover the increased risk, and as the demand for labor declines the price also declines. On the other hand, the proposition of the people, those who live by labor and traffic, is to extend the volume of currency, thereby cheapening money, and so stimulating manufacturing and other industries into such activity as will insure employment to the laboring classes at remunerative rates of wages. No contest was ever more clearly defined. At no time in the history of our country, not even in the history of the rebellion, has it been more evident that the interest of the many clash with those of the few.

It would seem from this view of the case that Senator Sherman, at first, was on the side of the people, but that the side of the oppressor became more fascinating to him, for some reason almost obvious to common mortals.

The contraction of the currency was not at first a Republican measure. It was bitterly opposed by the leading Republicans of the time and for years afterward. They condemned it in the severest terms. Senator Sherman said "it would be an act of folly without example for evil in modern times." Senator Wade said it would be "as bad as a fire." And in 1874, when the country was struggling with bankruptcy and general distress, Senator Logan said : " It is a money famine and nothing else."

I do not speak at random. Mr. Rutherford B. Hayes, afterward Republican President of the United States, has told us all about how contraction was enacted while he and the best Republicans voted against it.

In his speech at Sydney, Ohio, September 4, 1867, Mr. Hayes said :

> The very measure which was intended to carry out this policy of Secretary McCullough's, to enable him to take up the greenback currency with interest-bearing bonds, was introduced into Congress in March, 1866. I have here the votes upon that question, and I say that the Democratic party in both Houses—all the members of the Democratic Party in both Houses—voted for Secretary McCullough's plan, and that Mr. Jullian, Judge Schofield, Mr. Lawrance—all of whom I see here—and myself, a majority of the Republican members, voted against the scheme, and it became a law because a minority of the Union Party, with a unanimous vote of the Democratic Party, supported it, and because, when it was submitted to Andrew Johnson, instead of vetoing it as he did all Union Party measures, he wrote his name on the 12th of April at the bottom : " Approved, Andrew Johnson." I think, then, I am authorized in saying that these gentlemen are mistaken when they accuse the Union Party of being in favor of taking up the greenback currency and putting in the place of it interest-bearing, non-taxable bonds.—Howard's Life of Hayes, p. 206.

And that scheme, opposed by all true Union men at the time, including Senator Sherman, the same Senator now says, is one of the "great pillars of out financial credit."

Senator Logan continues the discussion of contraction as follows :

> It was the contraction and increased want of currency, and not a superabundance, which produced the necessity for running in debt, of which there is so much said on this floor. Why, sir, the people were never freer from debt in proportion to the business done than in 1865, at the close of the war, when Mr. McCullough began his system of contraction, and at the very time eleven millions more people were to be supplied. Was it to be supposed that the activity and energy which the adequate supply of money had put into operation, and which was giving prosperity and happiness to the country, would suddenly dwarf itself to suit financial notions without a severe struggle ? The inevitable result was an expedient to meet the consequent want, and credit was expanded. At the very moment, above all others, when adequate supply was needed, the opposite course was adopted ; and right hear lies the true cause of the late panic, which resulted from a money famine, and not from an excessive supply.

Senator Logan discusses the subject still further, as follows :

> Sir, turn this matter as we will, and look at it from any side whatever, and it does present the appearance of being a stupendous scheme [Mrs. Emery calls it a conspiracy] of the moneyholders to seize this opportunity of placing under their control the vast industries of the nation. Therefore I warn Senators against pushing too far the great conflict now going on between capital and labor. It is not our duty to legislate exclusively for either, but, as far as possible, to try and harmonize the interests of the two. Capital rests upon labor ; but when it attempts to press too heavily upon that which supports it in a free Republic, the slumbering volcano, whose mutterings are beginning already to be heard, will burst forth with a fury that no legislation will quell.

The Senator quotes and approves the following from the Berrien County (Mich.) *Record* :

> It is a lamentable fact that the financial question is leading to a conflict between capital and labor, money and production. The capitalists, the possessors of money, who stand isolated from the laboring and producing classes, are getting themselves in hostile array to oppose with might and main every effort to increase the currency of this country to something like an equal ratio with other commercial nations. The East, especially the Wall Streeters and banks, want no more money. They prefer to have the volume of currency limited so that combinations may be entered into and the money cornered. Every time a few millions of the currency are locked up in the East, the West suffers, the products of the West decline in price,

and the Western producer suffers, while the Eastern capitalist makes money. The time has come when this state of affairs should and must be remedied. The interest of the South and West are identical on this point, and, unless the East will yield to that which is just and right, the result cannot be otherwise than disastrous in the end. This the money-lenders of New York will learn, but, perhaps, not until it is too late.

I have dwelt at length on this subject of contraction because it is the central "Conspiracy" around which the others cluster, and because the greatest traitor of the day denies its existence. I will ask attention to but one more Republican statement and contradiction :

> If I were deciding this case upon what I considered the best evidence, I would be bound to say that I believed the money in actual circulation did not much, if at all, exceed $500,000,000, * * * or a trifle over $8 per capita.—*P.B. Plumb in United States Senate, June 1890.*

Mr. J.K. Hudson, a leading Republican editor, in April, 1890, stated that the amount of currency at one time was $2,242,576,028.41, "a per capita circulation of $64 at the close of the war, July 1, 1865."

I leave the stalwarts to settle their diverse statements in their own way. It seems as if the Republicans had recently entered into a bold conspiracy to deceive the people on this money question, even though they made themselves ridiculous by eating their own words and by contradicting each other.

The First "Conspiracy," wounding the greenback, was to enable the great fund-holders of the world to obtain United States bonds on easy terms. The Second, known as the national banking system, was to make the bonds very profitable to the holders, enabling them to draw double interest on one investment. The Third Conspiracy was to render money so scarce that the bonds would, probably, not be paid, making the investment perpetual.

The conspiracy of 1869 was to make the bonds payable in coin only, so that their payment would be still more burdensome and less probable.

It was with considerable difficulty that Congress passed the laws of 1869 and 1870, making the 5-20 currency bonds payable in coin, and refunding bonds so that no future Congress could undo the work. Those measures were vehemently opposed and condemned by John Sherman, Senator Doolittle, Oliver P. Morton, Henry Wilson and others. Senator Sherman called the Act of 1869 "extortion and repudiation." Senator Morton said that, "in its passage, four distinct laws were violated !" But the money power was all-powerful. It was unscrupulous, and, of course, it again triumphed.

In 1873 a coinage law was passed for the coinage of trade dollars and subsidiary silver. It in no way referred to the standard dollar, which had been the unit of account and the standard of value since the beginning of the government. It was an innocent and useful law, yet on this law was founded a "revision," adopted in bulk, June, 1874, as follows :

> The silver coins of the United States shall be a legal tender at their nominal value for any amount not exceeding $5 in any one payment.

That language demonetized all the silver coins of the United States for amounts above $5, including the standard silver dollar. The United States Monetary Commission Report of 1877, Vol. I, page 90, says :

> No law was ever passed by Congress of which this language can be considered a revision.

The report then adds :

> Whoever may be responsible for this error in the Revised Statutes, the ancient money of the country, instead of being intentionally legislated out of existence by Congress, was revised out of existence.

The law of 1875—the Resumption Law—was intended to redeem and retire the remaining greenbacks, making gold coin the money of the rich bondholders, and bank currency and subsidiary silver the moneys of trade and business. But the sufferings of the people and danger to the peace of the country became so great that Congress, in 1878, passed a law that redeemed greenbacks would not be canceled, but should be paid out again. This defeated the resumption scheme and saved to the people $346,000,000 of greenbacks. Another law was passed in 1878 restoring the full legal-tender quality of the silver dollar, and requiring its coinage at the rate of two to four millions per month. These were the first financial laws passed in the interests of the people since 1862. They were the first check to the money power since the passage of the exception clause on the greenback, which Thaddeus Stevens pronounced "the first victory of the money power over the country."

The remedial laws of 1878 were an immediate and immense relief to the people, showing that General Logan was right when he called the period from 1873 to 1878 "a money famine and nothing else."

The great Wall Street Journals were very much disgusted with the passage of the remedial measures of 1878. They unanimously ascribed their passage to the influence of the greenback sentiment of the West and South.

I have now sketched the manner and spirit of the enactment of the "Conspiracies" of the great money power of London and New York against the liberties of the American people, robbing them, with unseen hands, through the manipulations of the finances, as no highwaymen of ancient of modern times could have done it. And these are the crimes which Senator John Sherman says "are the seven great pillars of our financial credit."

The Senator denies that he ever had any interest in the First National Bank of New York. Of course it cannot be proven that he had. But circumstances are a little suspicious against him. I have on my table a "Political Manual" for 1880. Discussing "Secretary Sherman's Favorite Financial Agency," on page 146, I find this remark :

> The deposits controlled by the First National Bank [New York] were equal to nearly two and one-half times the entire deposits in all of the other seventy banks where such deposits were held.

Now if Senator Sherman was not financially interested in the First National Bank of New York, why did he thus favor it with the deposits of public moneys when he was Secretary of the Treasury under President Hayes ? Why should that particular bank receive deposits in the year 1878, from April to December, amounting to much more than all the other fiscal banks of the country ? I ask in all candor, whether the circumstances are not suspicious against the Senator ? Or was this conspiracy with that bank another "great pillar of our country's financial credit ?" We have the Senator's statement that there has been no contraction of the currency since the war, and that he never had any pecuniary interest in his pet bank. But the facts and circumstances against him in both cases are rather ugly ! He will next tell us, perhaps, that he became a millionaire by the honest savings from his salary as a public officer !

JOHN DAVIS.
Member of Congress from Kansas.

John DAVIS, 1826-1901

DAVIS, John. a Representative from Kansas ; born near Springfield, Sangamon County, Ill., August 9, 1826 ; moved with his parents to Macon County in 1830 ; attended the country schools, Springfield Academy, and Illinois College, Jacksonville, Ill. ; engaged in agricultural and horticultural pursuits near Decatur, Ill. ; moved to Kansas in 1872 and located on a farm near Junction City ; secretary of the Central Kansas Horticultural Society for many years ; elected president of the first distinctive farmers' convention held in Kansas in 1873, out of which grew the Farmers' Cooperative Association, of which he was the first president ; president of the Grange convention in 1874 ; became proprietor and editor of the Junction City Tribune in 1875 ; unsuccessful candidate of the Greenback Party for election in 1880 to the Forty-seventh Congress and in 1882 to the Forty-eighth Congress ; elected as a Populist to the Fifty-second and Fifty-third Congresses (March 4, 1891-March 3, 1895) ; unsuccessful candidate for reelection in 1894 to the Fifty-fourth Congress ; devoted his time to literary work until his death in Topeka, Kans., August 1, 1901 ; interment in Topeka Cemetery.

THE AUTHOR'S REVIEW OF SHERMAN

FOSTORIA, O., Oct. 16, 1891.

HON. JOHN SHERMAN :

My attention has just been called to your criticism of Seven Financial Conspiracies in the Cincinnati Enquirer of the 15th inst. You say you "first read the book with amusement and astonishment." I am not surprised at your astonishment when you see the enormity of your acts summed up and presented to the people in a plain, matter-of-fact way and that it should afford you amusement is only in keeping with a character that could deliberately plan such diabolisms. History tells us that "Nero fiddled while Rome burned," and history may tell posterity that John Sherman was "amused" when he saw his hellish schemes consummating in the overthrow of the American Republic.

You say the Seven Financial Conspiracies are "the seven great measures by which the country was saved from the perils of civil war," and yet you know that five of these laws were not enacted until after the war had closed. Senator, do you suppose you can make the people believe that the Contraction of the currency in 1866, the Credit-Strengthening Act of 1869, the Refunding Act of 1870, the Demonetization of Silver in 1873, or the Resumption Act of 1878 were measures instituted to save the country from a war that had successfully terminated in 1865 ? You certainly cannot deceive the people by this specious argument, and if you would deceive them in this, what reliance can be placed on your other statements ?

You say "the civil war was organized by slave-holders." It is true they were charged with the crime, but what of Wall Street and the notorious Zach Chandler, who openly asserted that "a country is not worth a damn without bloodletting," and who, through the agency of the civil war, was elevated from "a man of moderate means" to a position of a millionaire ; and, Senator, if I am correctly informed, Zachariah was not the only loyal northern man whose wealth was increased to phenomenal proportions through this infernal agency.

You say it is the men whom I denounce as "Shylocks" who furnished the means for carrying on the war. Ah, did they ? You know it was because they demanded such extortionate rates of interest for their money that the government resorted to the issuance of its own money, and you know that it was this very government money—the green back—that saved the country in the hour of peril. In your speech at Toledo on the evening of the 14th inst., you expatiated admirably upon the fact that "all our money is now as good as gold," but in speaking of the greenback you only parenthetically and stammeringly stated "true, it was depreciated for a time." Why did you not then and there tell your audience of the blighting effects of this depreciation and subsequent appreciation of the greenback on the wealth producers of the country ? Why did you pass so hurriedly over a question of such vital importance ? Sir, your object was to deceive the people, and it would be impossible in the same length of time to make more misleading and deceptive statements than you made on that occasion. It is no wonder that cunningly devised utterances choked in your throat. The most ordinary intelligence, not blinded by party prejudice, could easily detect the gauzy web you had so ingeniously prepared to entrap the unwary multitude. But, sir, the multitudes are becoming familiar with your deceptive arguments, and a righteously indignant people are rising to hurl from our national temple the heartless moneychangers who have torn our liberties from their shrine and are bartering them away to the enemies of freedom.

You acknowledge that the greenback was purposely depreciated to make a market for interest-bearing bonds. Why did you not also state an equally patent fact that it was to create a market for the gold which Shylock had hoarded in order that he might speculate upon the dire necessities of the country ?

Under the head of the first conspiracy you say "the duty on imported goods was required to be paid in coin in order to provide the means to pay the interest on our bonds in coin." But you previously stated that "the men who furnished the means to put down the rebellion were included among the most patriotic citizens of the northern states." Senator, was it an evidence of patriotism on the part of these *loyal* citizens to demand that the interest on the bonds which they had purchased with depreciated greenbacks should be paid in gold ? You insult every old veteran when you compare the patriotism of the gold kings in Wall Street with that of the soldier who faced death at the cannon's mouth and received in payment money which you say was purposely depreciated to create a market for bonds, the interest upon which was paid in gold when it required more than two dollars of the soldier's money to purchase one dollar of the bond-holder's money.

Under the head of second conspiracy you reiterate the thread-bare assertion that "the national bank system is the best that has ever been devised." This is the first time for more than twelve months that I have found a man sufficiently audacious to presume so much upon the ignorance of the people. The fact is, the people are becoming enlightened upon the vital questions of the day, and such perfidious statements fall powerless and harmless even from the lips of a United States Senator.

Under the head of the third conspiracy—contraction—you assert that "from the beginning of the war until the present time our volume of money has been increasing year by year more rapidly than our population." And if I remember correctly you stated in your Toledo speech that we now have more money per capita than ever before. You also charge that my statements in regard to the contraction of the currency "are not only misleading, but absolutely false." Now let us see if it is not Senator Sherman who is attempting to mislead the people. The entire controversy in regard to our money volume arises from the fact that the manipulators of our finances find the people awakening to their corrupt methods, and in order to retain public confidence it has become necessary to cover up the iniquities of past legislation. To do this you now claim that the 7-30 treasury notes and compound interest notes were not money. But Secretary McCullough,

Treasurer T.E. Spinner and Senator John A. Logan concurred in counting compound interest and the 7-30 notes as a part of the currency. Indeed, they were made lawful money and a *legal tender* by the acts creating them. General Spinner, in reply to a letter of inquiry written Aug. 17, 1876, says : " The 7-30 notes were intended, prepared, issued and used, as money," and scores of people are still living who will testify that these notes passed current as money. And, Senator, the fact that today you come before the people stating that they were not money is unmistakable evidence of the crafty methods you have adopted to gull and mislead a confiding people. You say that what I call money was "the most burdensome form of interest-bearing securties at 7 3-10 percent interest." Well, this interest was payable in the same kind of money and ceased altogether at the end of three years.

Will you figure out how much was saved to the tax payers by exchanging these 7-30 notes for 5-20s bearing gold interest at 6 per cent. With fifty cents in gold the bond holder purchased $1.00 of these 5-20s bearing gold interest; now did he not really get 6 per cent in gold on his fifty cent gold investment, or 12 per cent on the investment that cost him but $1.00 in gold ? While his means were invested in the 7-30s he received but 7 3-10 per cent in paper but after investing in the 5-20s he received 6 per cent in gold equivalent to 12 per cent in paper on the investment which cost him but fifty cents in gold. Senator will you please tell us how it is that 12 per cent is less burdensome than 7 3-10 per cent ? Evidently you have figured on the basis presented by Maj. McKinley " That a mortgage is an evidence of prosperity," from which standpoint you reach the logical conclusion that the higher the rate of interest the greater the degree of prosperity. Woe unto you hypocrites who under the pretense of relieving the people double their burdens and perpetuate their bondage.

In order to complete your deception, you attempt to still further deceive the people by manipulating the Treasurer's Report in such a manner as to make it appear that we now have a larger per capita circulation than at any previous time. This has been done first by including in our present circulation the entire amount of greenbacks $346,000,000 which were only saved from the cremation furnace through the efforts of a few sturdy greenbackers led by our invincible Weaver and the great souled Peter Cooper. Now you know that thousands and even millions of that money have been destroyed during the past twenty-eight years by fire, flood and the natural agencies of destruction. Secretray Foster includes in his (campaign) report the various national and private bank reserves which every body knows avails nothing to our depressed industrial classes. No amount of money locked up in treasury and bank vaults could bring relief to the people. An abundant and healthy circulating medium is as necessary to national life as blood is to physical life. The body of a hanged man has an abundance of blood but its stagnation caused him to die. So when a nation's circulating medium stagnates in bank vaults or is disproportionately shrunken in volume that nation will as surely die. The testimony of Secretary McCullough, Spinner, Logan, Plumb and other leading authorities bear me out in the assertion that our actual per capita circulation is less than one fourth that of 1866. As proof of this Secretary McCullough in his report for Dec. 1865 says we have now about $2,000,000,000 nearly all in circulation among the people.

Our population at that time was 35,000,000 consequently we had about $57 per capita. Secretary Foster in his report for campaign purposes in 1891 shows about $1,588,000,000 with a population of 64,000,000 which gives per capita circulation of over $24. Secretary Foster, however, in his anxiety to present a winning campaign document deceives the people by omitting the important fact that nearly one half the amount is not in circulation. A fair estimate shows the

```
Loss of paper money during 28 years ........ . .. $ 50,000,000
hoarded-low estimate ......................................... 25,000,000
National bank reserves—Comp. report 1889, p. 51...460,000,000
Private bank reserves-estimated ...................... 250,000,000
................................................................................785,000,000
Balance in actual circulation $803,000,000.
Population ...............................64,000,000.
Per capita in circulation...................$12.50.
```

This calculation is far more liberal than that of Senator Plumb who in 1890 said the circulation did not exceed $500,000,000, or a little more than $8 per capita.

You say that my statements in regard to this matter "are palpable falsehoods, and if stated by a man would justify a stronger word." Very well, Senator, use your strongest language, but please apply it where it belongs, to your colleagues, Secretary McCullough, Spinner, Logan and Plumb. You say you were not in favor of contraction of the greenbacks and made a speech against it. I am aware of that fact, and made a quotation from your speech showing that your views were correct on this subject. At the same time we find you in 1875 passing the Resumption Act, which provided for the destruction of every dollar of that money. Your views were also correct when in 1866 you said "the bondholder can demand only the kind of money he paid. He is a repudiator and extortioner to demand money more valuable than he gave." Now if this view was correct in 1866, was it not equally correct in 1879 ? Then why did you, in a speech made in Toledo in that year say "that to refuse to pay the bonds in gold would be repudiation and extortion, and would be scoffing at the blessings of Almighty God." Senator the fact that your worldly possessions were wonderfully augmented during these years justifies a very general suspicion that you had fallen into "ways that were dark, etc."

Under the fourth head—the Credit-Strengthening Conspiracy—you say, "I maintain and still believe that by a fair construction of the Loan Law we had a right to pay the principal of the bonds as they matured in greenbacks of the kind and character in existence when the bonds were issued." Now this is precisely the ground I take in regard to this matter, therefore I see no occassion for controversy upon this subject ; though it is universally conceded that through this act of Congress, which you supported, the people were robbed of hundreds of millions of dollars, and will ever be denounced as one of the most diabolical conspiracies in the record of crime.

The Refunding Act was simply a scheme to perpetuate the national debt, and no amount of glamour or sophistry will make it appear otherwise in the minds of a debt-ridden and tax cursed people.

Your claim that the bonds were refunded to secure a lower rate of interest is calculated solely to deceive the people. We have already shown that it was far easier for the people to pay 7 3-10 per cent interest with paper money depreciated one-half than it was to pay 6 per cent in gold interest. Senator, I agree with your "intelligent statesmen" that the Refunding Act "was a measure of the highest value conducted with remarkable success." It certainly was a measure of highest value to the bond-holders, and conducted with remarkable success by their agents of which you appear as chief.

Under the head of Demonetization of Silver you again resort to your "honest dollar" deception, and attempt to terrorize the farmer, the laborer and the soldier by the fear that they are going to be paid off in "dishonest dollars." Senator, if we have any "dishonest dollars" was it not a Republican congress under your manipulations that made them so ? Are you deterred from taking a silver dollar because there is only seventy-seven cents worth of silver in it ? You say it will buy as much and is equally as good as the gold dollar, the national bank note or the greenback. Will you sell your silver dollars for seventy-seven cents ? Certainly not, for they are worth one hundred cents in the market. Then why attempt to confuse and prejudice the soldier by telling him that he will be paid in "cheap dollars," "dishonest dollars," "short dollars," etc., unless your party wins ?

This solicitude in regard to the soldier, however, seems quite out of character on your part when we reflect that while our country was in the throes of civil war, it was through such legislation as you prescribed that the soldier was paid in a currency which you say was depreciated in order to make a market for gold-interest bearing bonds. This "dishonest dollar," over which you have so long and loudly lamented, has no exception clause upon it. You boast that our money is all equally good, that one kind of a dollar will buy as much as another kind. Since this is true, why do you attempt to deceive the people by this talk of "dishonest dollars ?" Money can only be dishonest when its purchasing power is impaired. If we have ever had any dishonest money it was that which Congress depreciated by placing the exception clause upon it and then compelled the soldier in the field to accept it for his services. And, sir, did not you, under the instruction of a London banker, Earnest Seyd, manipulate this legislation— Demonetization of Silver—in the interests of British and American capitalists ? Senator Ingalls says in his great speech, in the U.S. Senate, Jan. 14, 1891, "there is a deep-seated conviction among the people, which I fully share, that the demonetization of silver in 1873 was one element of a great conspiracy to deliver the fiscal system of this country over to those by whom it has in my opinion finally been captured. * * * So great was the power of capital, so profound was the impulse, so persistent was the determination, the promoters of this scheme succeeded by the operation of mind power and will force in capturing and bewildering the intelligence of men of all parties, of members of both houses of congress, the members of the cabinet and the president of the United States. * * * As I say, it is one of the phenomena and anomalies of legislation, and I have no other explanation to make than this : I believe that both houses of congress and the president of the United States must have been hypnotized." Senator, were you hypnotized on that memorable occasion ? Excuse this seemingly personal and impertinent question, for the truth is, British gold and Washington whiskey have been such important factors in American legislation during the past thirty years that one is hardly able to determine whether this was or was not a genuine case of hypnotization. You claim however, that you understood this measure was before congress. It was no secret with you. You evidently were not hypnotized. The management of such a stupendous conspiracy necessitated a clear brain and an unyielding nerve. You, doubtless, were the great hypnotizer.

Under the head of Resumption you claim this crowning act to be the "glory and pride of the people of the United States." You extol our credit, our productive interests, the development of our national resources, but not one word have you to say of the general advancement and prosperity of the masses. The truth is, under your "beneficent financial policy" the masses are being rapidly reduced to a condition of wage slavery. With 9,000,000 of mortgaged homes, $30,000,000,000 of indebtedness, and one-half the wealth of the country in the hands of 31,000 people, the boast of prosperity is a mockery, and an insult to common intelligence.

S.E.V. EMERY.

The Press and People Endorse It.

OFFICE OF DR. ALBERT FULLER,
KIRWIN, KAN., December 10, 1888.

The little book, "Seven Financial Conspiracies" by Mrs. S.E.V. Emery, is a warning voice. It reveals the destructive tendency of corrupt legislation in our country. It should be carefully read and well considered by every American citizen. CORRUPTIONISTS may HISS at it, but HISTORY will HONOR the WOMAN who WROTE it.

ALBERT FULLER, M.D.

OFFICE OF THE KANSAS COMMONER,
NEWTON, KANSAS, Dec. 13, 1888.

MRS. S.E.V. EMERY :

DEAR MADAM—Your little work, "Seven Financial Conspiracies," has been of wonderful service in the late campaign in Kansas. It was called the " Union Labor Bible," and was read by most of the farmers in this portion of the state ; a profound impression was produced by its teachings which will remain as the basis of future victory. Many for the first time caught a glimpse of the profound facts connected with financial slavery, and although thousands who have been convicted of sin have so far failed to fully embrace the truth, still a foundation has been laid in the minds of the majority that will in the near future uphold the cause of "the great plain people."

I sincerely hope that its circulation may be most widely extended.

Very truly,
J.R. ROGERS.

The person who is not thoroughly well informed upon the cause that has, within the last twenty years, produced five thousand millionaires, while producing one million tramps and fixing death-grip " mortgages" on over one-half the homes of America, should buy and read this little book, and be wise in time to prevent the further aggression of monopolies.—Weekly Review, Douglasville, Ga.

What you have revealed is startling and makes me think of what John the Revelator saw. I have set others to reading it and they are all as much surprised as I am.—MRS. GEO. STEBBINS.

In my estimation you are fully entitled to the first premium for a work adapted for general circulation among the masses. You have done your work well ; God bless you.—J.M. CALKINS.

SEVEN FINANCIAL CONSPIRACIES WHICH HAVE ENSLAVED THE AMERICAN PEOPLE.—The above is the title of an invaluable little book of eighty-five pages, graphically written, in a concise form, though the whole story is told ; and ought to be read by every man, woman and child living in the United States. We are not able to find language to express thanks to our noble sister for her grand work.—The National Review.

Your little book has come to me like a revelation from the ever living God—Leon Lewis.

I learned more in relation to the financial history of our country during the past thirty years, by reading carefully Mrs. S.E.V. Emery's "Seven Financial Conspiracies," than I had ever known before. I advise every voter to lay aside prejudice and read this wonderful little book. JOHN P. ST. JOHN. Ex-Governor of Kansas.

I received from Washington, some time ago, the report of the United States silver commission and find it a grand document for the American people. In perusing its pages I underscored the passages that struck me as being especially significant and important, with a lead pencil, and now have before me a grand, italicized, governmental, Union Labor, campaign document, issued by Congress at Washington.

It looked so nice, laying thus before me, that I thought the plan would be a good one with some of our other best authors.

It worked well till I come to Mrs. S.E.V. Emery's "Seven Financial Conspiracies." Here I was completely surprised and nonplussed. I found my pencil instinctively running under every line, and from one side of the page to the other, without being able to discriminate as to which words or thoughts were more weighty than the others. For superlative excellence in everything that she lays her hand to give me a woman. With this thought I dropped my pencil with the exclamation : My God, there is no danger of the American people being enslaved as long as they have such mothers as that !

Give women the ballot and they will send the liquor business higher than Gilderoy's kite. Give woman the ballot and the "Seven Financial Conspiracies" reviewed by Mrs. Emery and the seventy-seven other conspiracies by John Bull & Co. will melt away in the sunshine of her Superior and instinctive perception. She has more moral courage than man. Vide the late crusades in Missouri. She has a clearer perception of motives and proprieties than man. She rules the nation in its infancy and it would be all the better if her trained and experienced counsels, and the impulses of her more faithful and loving heart, were over her boys as long as they live. Women most always prove themselves equal to the emergency, no matter what that emergency may be.

The negro problem would soon be solved ; the financial troubles would disappear.

The country would, no doubt, gain immeasurably, by an unrestricted enfranchisement of our wives and mothers.

With the same constancy that arms her to repel intruders, in her domestic sphere, she would send John Bull home to attend to Ireland, India and Portugal, and warn him to keep his fingers out of our finances. "The poor ye have always with you," said Jesus, " and whensoever ye will ye may do them good." At last, in these latter days, God has given the poor a government, the Democratic Republic of America. The poor, being in the majority, have the reins of government always within their grasp. The rich, in this and other lands are endeavoring to steal away the government from the poor. Half the men are blind and do not see it. Women being more sensitive and the first to suffer, are keenly alive to these despicable methods. Let us arm the women to make a lawful crusade against our wrongs.

Hopefully yours.
—J.L. Switzer, in the Chicago Express.

HEADQUARTERS UNION LABOR PARTY.
CHETOPA, KAN., November 24, 1888.

Mrs. S.E.V. Emery, Lansing, Mich.:

MY DEAR MADAM—I believe the little book "Seven Financial Conspiracies," of which we distributed 60,000 copies, is entitled to more credit than all else in making Kansas the Banner Union Labor State. It has caused more men, both Democrat and Republican, to investigate the financial legislation of the country, than any other document of its size ever brought before the reading public.

Very truly yours,
JNO. W. BREIDENTHAL,
Chairman State Central Committee.

Not since the days of Uncle Tom's Cabin has a mere statement of facts drawn from the pages of history been subject to such severe scrutiny and vindictive criticism as has Mrs. Emery's little book, entitled "Seven Financial Conspiracies," &c., within the past six months.

During the presidential campaign over fifty thousand copies of this stirring document were circulated in the State of Kansas alone ; and so effective was its influence on the side of the people that it was made the special object of attack by the ablest speakers of the great monopoly party of the State, by organized central committees, and by the most powerful and widely circulated Journals of the great Wall street party.

Yet in all this fiery furnace of rage, vituperation, slander and abuse, not a break or a fracture was found in the harness of this glorious little book. Not a statement was disproved or a position overthrown. Republican speakers on the rostrum were seen to exhibit it to their audiences, to misread its pages, to use the most withering invectives in their denunciations, and then, in their rage, to dash it on the floor, to spit upon it and to stamp it with their feet !

A book worthy so much vindictive and apprehensive attention on the part of the enemies of popular liberty is no common production. This little book is, in our opinion, the most powerful and valuable document of its size now in use.—Junction City (Kan.) Tribune.

OFFICE OF THE AMERICAN NONCONFORMIST,
WINFIELD, KAN.

MRS. EMERY :

You observe that Kansas comes up with 10,000 more U.L. votes than any other State in the Union, and in justice it should be known that the little "Seven Shooter" was the greatest agency and the strongest lever brought into service. It called out the fire of the enemy as nothing else. We shall need 100,000 of them for 1889, for the U.L. Party means to save Kansas. The best thing outside of this State is the conversion of the St. Louis Christian Advocate, caused by the Editor reading your book. He comes out square and is now running a series of articles showing up the whole system. Let us take courage and keep up the fight.

Yours,
H. & L. VINCENT.
Publishers Nonconformist.

The people turned out en masse to do all honor to Mrs. S.E.V. Emery. The parade at 11:30 was immense. In the afternoon a very large and attentive audience gathered to listen to Mrs. Emery, who is one of the finest speakers it has ever been our good fortune to hear. For three hours she held her audience spellbound listening to the words of wisdom, eloquence and truth that she uttered ; her very appearance is a benediction. She is a grand, good woman and that vast crowd testified its appreciation by frequently interrupting her with cheers and cries of, "that's so," etc. After the speaking the audience dispersed with three cheers for Mrs. Emery—long may she live to continue her grand and noble work of educating and elevating mankind.—Stafford (Kansas), Advocate.

SHELBY, October 11, 1886.

ED. TRIBUNE—Say to the people of Oceans county, through your paper, that if they get a chance to hear Sarah E.V. Emery during her course of lectures in the county this week, to do so by all means. In our opinion, and we voice the sentiment of the Shelby people without regard to party, the Michigan lecture platform has on it no abler speaker today than Mrs. Emery. Pleasing in her delivery, clear cut and decisive in her argument, with a remarkably strong and pleasing voice, Mrs. Emery will hold an audience for two hours, so still that you can hear a pin drop. Her subject, "Whither are we drifting ?" is political but not partisan. Dealing with the great questions which today demand attention at the hands of the people in a fair, impartial manner, and suggesting the remedy which in her opinion is most concise and common sense. Her lectures are free to everybody.—Shelby Tribune (Shelby) Michigan.

The Seven Financial Conspiracies was the principle weapon used by the stalwart Kansans in their memorable war with and defeat of the "Irredescent Dreamer," John J. Ingalls. It is the best eye opener for the average voter now before the public and ought to be in the hands of every American citizen.

CHAS. N. BROWN,
Editor Alliance Defender.

No pamphlet published has struck such terrible and effective blows as has this one. The eighty-second thousand is ready to be sent out. It goes right back to the root of these great evils and shows in a manner that will convince, how the servility of the people is being brought about by deep laid and foul conspiracies which have been carried out, and are now daily gnawing at the vitals of the republic.—Non-Conformist, Winfield, Kansas.

Mrs. Emery is of large build, physically, mentally and spiritually. She possesses a superb voice, well trained in the elocutionist arts, poised by such superior mental powers and a knowledge of her subjects, that made her master of the occasion. We have no power of pen, or language at command to do anything like justice to her speech.

We have listened to Wendell Phillips, humanity's silver tongued orator ; to Henry Ward Beecher, the proud preacher of Plymouth church ; to John B. Gough ; to the forensic efforts of Roscoe Conklin and Carlisle ; to the brant productions of "Sunset Cox" and polish of Gen Weaver, but never in all did we listen to such a speech as delivered by Mrs. Emery to 5,000 people at the Knights of Labor celebration. July 4th, 1887. From first to last she held them spellbound by the magic of her orator, the clearness of her argument and power of her logic. We shall not even attempt a review. Suffice it to say that 5,000 people will never forget her burning words, portraying the wrongs that the wealth producers—the true business and laboring classes suffer under—and the true remedy—a national solution of the money question in the interests of those classes.—The People's Advocate, Independence, Iowa, July 7th, 1887.

Mrs. Emery's Success Upon the Rostrum.

At 2 p.m. the people gathered in Lafayette park, and listened to a long and interesting address by Mrs. Emery. The gathering was so large that not more than one-third of the people were able to hear the address. There were no newspaper men on the stand and a full report of the speech cannot be given. It is said to be one of the finest talks on the vital questions of the day made in Kansas this year. Mrs. Emery is a forcible writer and understands the history of our country as well as anyone that is on the public stage now. The talk was well received from first to last and made a good impression on the hearers.—Beacon, Great Bend, Kansas.

One of the largest audiences ever assembled in the court house greeted the lady speaker last evening. Mrs. Emery, besides being an orator, proved herself to be a master of her subject, and her command of language was somewhat amazing to those at least who think that a lady is not capable of delivering an address in public, more especially when the subject chosen deals with the great political questions of the day.—Abilene (Kansas) Gazette.

Mrs. S.E.V. Emery, a talented and interesting Union Labor lecturer, addressed a crowded house Tuesday evening. While we do not subscribe to the U.L. faith entirely, yet there is much to be commended in Mrs. E.'s speech, Her review of John Sherman and the relation his financial policy bears to the present stagnated condition of agriculture, her interpretations of the workings of the tariff laws, and the manner in which they have strangled labor, were unanswerable.—Girard Herald (Rep.) (Girard) Kansas.

Mrs. Emery, of Lansing, delivered an address in the Congregational church last Monday evening, under the auspices of the W.C.T.U. Her lecture was a very intellectual production. With a woman's pathetic pleading, she combine's the convincing logic of a strong reasoner and the persuasive power of a graceful orator. She speaks with great ease and fluency, and is thoroughly well posted.—Williamston Enterprise, (Williamston) Michigan.

Mrs. Emery is a lady of fine presence, has a clear and powerful voice and an easy and often eloquent oratory which gives her front rank among platform speakers. She handled her theme with great skill and made a strong impression in favor of woman suffrage as necessary not only to the cause of temperance and other vital reforms, but the perpetuation of republican government. Senator Peffer and Congressman Simpson were present and in short speeches unqualifiedly indorsed the arguments of Mrs. Emery and pledged their adhesion to the reforms she advocated.—Emporia Daily Gazette.

The late dailies contain Hon. John Sherman's sharp reply to that remarkably powerful and popular little book, "The Seven Financial Conspiracies." More than 100,000 copies of this book have been sold in the past year. No woman ever trod foot on Shelby county soil whose sweet, persuasive eloquence thrilled people with more righteous fervor than did the words of Mrs. Emery at Lithia Springs last August.—Our Best Words, Shelbyville, Ill., Nov 21,1891.

DECLARATION OF CONDITIONS.

[Adopted by the People's Party at Omaha, July 4, 1892.]

Assembled upon the one hundred and sixteenth anniversary of the declaration of independence, the People's Party of America, in their first national convention, invoking upon their action the blessing of Almighty God, puts forth in the name and on behalf of the people of this country the following preamble and declaration of principles :

The conditions which surround us justify our co-operation ; we meet in the midst of a nation brought to the verge of moral, political and material ruin. Corruption dominates the ballot box, the Legislature, the Congress, and touches even the ermine of the bench. The people are demoralized, most of the States have been compelled to isolate the voters at the polling places to prevent universal intimidation or bribery. The newspapers are largely subsidized or muzzled, public opinion silenced ; business prostrated ; our homes covered with mortgages ; labor impoverished and the land concentrating in the hands of the capitalists. The urban workmen are denied the right of organization for self-protection ; imported pauperized labor beats down their wages ; a hireling standing army, unrecognized by our laws, is established to shoot them down, and they are rapidly degenerating into European conditions. The fruit of the toil of millions are boldly stolen to build up colossal fortunes for a few, unprecedented in the history of mankind ; and the possessors of these, in turn, despise the republic and endanger liberty. From the same prolific womb of governmental injustice we breed the two great classes—tramps and millionaires.

The national power to create monopoly enriches bondholders ; a vast public debt payable in legal tender currency has been funded into gold-bearing bonds, thereby adding millions to the burdens of the people.

Silver, which has been accepted as coin since the dawn of history has been demonetized to add to the purchasing power of gold by increasing the value of all forms of property as well as human labor, and the supply of currency is purposely abridged to fatten usurers, bankrupt enterprise and enslave industry. A vast conspiracy against mankind has been organized on the two continents, and it is rapidly taking possession of the world. If not met and overthrown at once it forbodes terrible social convulsions, the destruction of civilization, or the establishment of despotism. We have witnessed for more than a quarter of a century the struggles of the two great political parties for power and plunder, while grievous wrongs have been inflicted upon the suffering people. We charge that the controlling influences dominating both these parties have permitted the extending dreadful conditions to develop without serious effort to prevent or restrain them. Neither do they now promise us any substantial reform. They have agreed together to ignore in the coming campaign every issue but one. They promise to drown the outcries of plundered people with the uproar of a sham battle over the tariff, so that capitalists, corporations, national banks, rings, trusts, watered stock, the demonetization of silver and the oppressions of the usurers may all be lost sight of. They propose to sacrifice our homes, lives and children on the altar of mammon ; to destroy the multitude in order to secure corruption funds from the millionaires.

Assembled on the anniversary of the birthday of the nation, and filled with the spirit of the grand generation who established our independence, we seek to restore the government of the republic to the hands of "the plain people" with whose class it originated. We assert our purposes to be identical with the purposes of the national Constitution, to form a more perfect union, and establish justice, insure domestic tranquility, provide for the common defense, promote the general welfare and secure the blessings of liberty or ourselves and our posterity.

We declare that this country can only endure as a free government while built upon the love of the whole people for each other and for the nation, that it cannot be pinned together by bayonets, that the civil war is over, and that every passion and resentment which grew out of it must die with it, and that we must be in fact as we are in name, one united brotherhood of free men.

Our country finds its future confronted with conditions for which there is no precedent in the history of the world. We pledge ourselves that if given power we will labor to correct these evils by wise and reasonable legislation in accordance with the terms of our platform.

We believe that the powers of government—in other words, of the people—should be expanded (as in the case of the postal service) as rapidly and as far as the good sense of an intelligent people and the teachings of experience shall justify, to the end that oppression, injustice and poverty shall eventually cease in the land.

While our sympathies as a party of reform are naturally on the side of every proposition which will tend to make men intelligent, virtuous and temperate, we nevertheless regard these questions—important as they are—as secondary to the issues now pressing for solution, and upon which not only our individual prosperity but the very existence of free institutions depend ; and we ask all men to first help us to determine whether we are to have a republic to administrate, before we differ as to the conditions upon which it is to be administered ; believing that the forces of reform this day organized will never cease to move forward until every wrong is remedied and equal rights and equal privileges securely established for all the men and women of this country.

PLATFORM OF PRINCIPLES

We declare that the union of the labor forces of the United States this day consummated shall be permanent and perpetual ; may its spirit enter into all hearts for the salvation of the republic, and the uplifting of mankind.

2. Wealth belongs to him who creates it, and every dollar taken from industry without an equivalent, is robbery. "If any will not work neither shall he eat." The interests of rural and civic labor are the same ; their enemies are identical.

3. We believe that the time has come when the railroad corporations will either own the people or the people must own the railroads, and should the government enter upon the work of owning and managing all roads, we should favor an amendment to the Constitution by which all persons engaged in the government service shall be placed under a civil service regulation of the most rigid character so as to prevent the increase of the power of the national administration by the use of such additional government employes.

FINANCE.

We demand a national currency, safe, sound and flexible, issued by the general government only, a full legal tender for all debts, public and private, and that without the issue of banking corporations ; a just, equitable and efficient means of distribution direct to the people at a tax not to exceed 2 per cent. per annum to be provided as set forth in the sub-treasury plan of the Farmers' Alliance, or a better system ; also by payments in discharge of its obligations for public improvements.

We demand free and unlimited coinage of silver and gold at the present legal ratio of 16 to 1.

We demand that the amount of circulating medium be speedily increased to not less than $50 per capita.

We demand a graduated income tax.

We believe that the money of the country should be kept as much as possible in the hands of the people, and hence we demand that all state and national revenues shall be limited to the necessary expenses of the government economically and honestly administered.

We demand that postal savings banks be established by the government for the safe deposit of the earnings of the people, and to facilitate exchange.

TRANSPORTATION.

Transportation being a means of exchange and a public necessity, the government should own and operate the railroads in the interests of the people.

The telegraph, telephone, like the postoffice system, being a necessity for the transmission of news, should be owned and operated by the government in the interest of the people.

LAND.

The land, including all the natural resources of wealth, is the heritage of the people and should not be monopolized for speculative purposes, and alien ownership of land should be prohibited. All land now held by railways and other corporations in excess of their actual needs, and all lands now owned by aliens, should be reclaimed by the government and held for actual settlers only.